Swarnalatha A, Sharmila K, Akash A V (Eds.)

Exploring New Horizon in Research

Swarnalatha A, Sharmila K, Akash A V (Eds.)

Exploring New Horizon in Research

LAP LAMBERT Academic Publishing

Imprint

Any brand names and product names mentioned in this book are subject to trademark, brand or patent protection and are trademarks or registered trademarks of their respective holders. The use of brand names, product names, common names, trade names, product descriptions etc. even without a particular marking in this work is in no way to be construed to mean that such names may be regarded as unrestricted in respect of trademark and brand protection legislation and could thus be used by anyone.

Cover image: www.ingimage.com

Publisher:
LAP LAMBERT Academic Publishing
is a trademark of
Dodo Books Indian Ocean Ltd. and OmniScriptum S.R.L publishing group

120 High Road, East Finchley, London, N2 9ED, United Kingdom
Str. Armeneasca 28/1, office 1, Chisinau MD-2012, Republic of Moldova, Europe
Managing Directors: Ieva Konstantinova, Victoria Ursu
info@omniscriptum.com

Printed at: see last page
ISBN: 978-620-8-44283-5

Exploring New Horizons in Research

Edited by

Swarnalatha A
Sharmila K
Akash A V

Foreword

In an age defined by rapid change and continuous innovation, the role of research has never been more critical. It is through inquiry, discovery, and the courage to explore the unknown that science drives progress and shapes the future. The title **"Exploring New Horizons in Research"** captures the very essence of this pursuit—an intellectual journey that transcends disciplines, challenges conventions, and opens doors to novel possibilities.

This volume stands as a testament to the evolving nature of scientific exploration. It highlights emerging fields, innovative methodologies, and transformative ideas that are reshaping the research landscape. Each chapter serves as a window into areas that were once on the periphery but are now moving to the forefront, offering fresh perspectives and groundbreaking insights.

"Exploring New Horizons in Research" is more than just a compilation of topics; it is an invitation to think differently and to innovate fearlessly. It is a valuable resource for scholars, researchers, and students alike—those who seek not only to understand the present but to shape the future.

CHAPTERS

CHAPTER 1

NUTRITIONAL AND FUNCTIONAL VALUES JACK FRUIT

Rafa Anver K

Department of Food Science and Nutrition, Nehru Arts and Science College, Coimbatore, Tamil Nadu-641 105

Introduction:

The jackfruit grows in the tropical lowlands of South and Southeast Asia, and it is native to the rain forests of the Western Ghats of India. Brazil and Central and Eastern Africa. Bangladesh, India, Myanmar, Thailand, Vietnam, China, the Philippines, Indonesia, Malaysia, and Sri Lanka are the main producers of jackfruit. In Southern Asia and other warm nations in both hemispheres, it is a popular and reasonably priced fruit. India is regarded as the jackfruit's motherland and is the world's second-largest producer. It is widely distributed throughout India, including the foothills of the Himalayas, Assam, Tripura, Bihar, Uttar Pradesh, and the southern Indian states of Kerala, Tamil Nadu, and Karnataka.

One of India's biggest producers of jackfruit is Tamil Nadu. 2,936 hectares are used for jackfruit cultivation overall. The largest area under jackfruit is in the Cuddalore district, which is followed by Kanyakumari and Dindigul, with 682 hectares, 650 hectares, and 429 hectares, respectively.

In every region of India, commercial jack fruit agriculture is still in its infancy, and farmers are even ignorant of the more advanced growing techniques. Jack production, harvesting, and commercialization provide a variety of challenges for farmers. They must deal with uncertainty and other natural disasters like drought and cyclones during the cultivation stage. One of the issues taken into consideration during farming is water constraint. Because fruits are perishable, a large portion of them are wasted during the harvesting stage because there are insufficient storage facilities and ineffective processing or preservation methods. Fruit damage results from a lack of skilled labor for harvesting. During the marketing stage, they deal with issues like pricing volatility, a lack of current and trustworthy market data, an improper grading system or standardization, and an inadequate institutionalized marketing infrastructure. (Chandrakanth Reddy, C. Prabakar, K. Sita Devi, T. Ponnarasi and Y. Shelton Peter *et al,* 2019)

Biological Classification:

Jackfruit, a tropical fruit belonging to the genus Artocarpus and family Moraceae, is typically favored because of its delicately sweet flavor. Nonetheless, vegans and vegetarians find this fruit's remarkable nutritional profile to be on par with shredded meat. Jackfruit is different from other fruits since it has a lot of fiber, vitamins, minerals, antioxidants, low fats, and protein (more than 3 grams per cup). Jackfruit is grown in a variety of climates, with the exception of the temperate zone.

Nutritional Value

Around the world, a number of well-liked jackfruit types are available. A variety of propagation techniques were used to produce uniformly healthy jackfruit seedlings. In order to improve fruit output, jackfruit is grown using a number of cultural methods, including training, pruning, weed control, fertilizer management, and irrigation management. This chapter's introduction, summary of fruit crops, production, consumption, nutritional value, cultural customs around jackfruit, and cost-benefit analysis were all attempted in this study.

Nutritional Value is rich in dietary fiber, vitamins (including C and B6), and minerals (such potassium and magnesium), jackfruit is regarded as a nutrient-dense fruit. Customers are now more interested in jackfruit as a nutritious food choice because of its nutritional profile. Culinary Versatility of jackfruit can be used in a wide range of culinary applications due to its distinct flavor and texture. Because of its fibrous, meat-like texture, it is frequently used as a vegetarian or vegan meat alternative in stir-fries, tacos, sandwiches, and curries. The culinary appeal of jackfruit is increased by its versatility in both savory and sweet preparations. It is a sustainable crop. Jackfruit trees are renowned for their adaptability to a variety of agroclimatic circumstances. They can adapt to a variety of soil types and require comparatively few inputs. Farmers find it to be a desirable crop since it can be cultivated organically and supports sustainable agricultural methods. Farmers, producers, and exporters can benefit financially from the commercial cultivation of jackfruit. There are now opportunities for employment and revenue development in the agriculture industry due to the rising demand for jackfruit and its products both domestically and abroad. (Rakhi Goutam and Km Kusum *et al.,* 2020)

Origin and Classification:

Originating in East Asia, jackfruit is the largest fruit produced by trees. It may weigh up to 30 kg and produces 50–80 tons per hectare per year. The fruit has been employed on a modest and crude basis in value-added products, but it has a lot of potential in Uganda. In order to ascertain the jackfruit's ability to support industrial-scale processing, this study evaluated its production and consumption trends. From April to June 2016, a cross-sectional survey was carried out in areas that produce jackfruit. The size of a household farm, the quantity of jackfruit trees, their varieties, methods of use, and the limitations related to jackfruit production were the variables under investigation. To choose districts, sub-counties, parishes, and villages to take part in the survey, a purposive sample design was employed. A semi-structured questionnaire was used to interview 400 household heads from the study area. In addition to recording observations and responses, secondary data was examined to determine the overall number of houses in a district. According to the findings, 32% of those surveyed worked on farms with 1-2 acres and at least 2–7 jackfruit trees. Of the jackfruit trees, 43% were inherited and the remaining 57% were planted. An estimated 1.7 million fruiting jackfruit trees with an average fruit weight of 11 kg and a fruit count ranging from 20 to 120 per tree were found in the study region. March to April and November to December are Uganda's two jackfruit harvest season peaks, with the later producing more fruit. Based on the color of the pulp, jackfruit is classified as white, orange, or yellow. The pulp texture determines whether the fruit is hard or soft. Approximately 78% of households grew jack fruit primarily for their own food, 16% sold it, 6% fed it to animals, and 1% turned it into jackfruit wine or dry chips. In the research region, 0.3 million metric tons of jackfruit were produced annually each district. In order to meet the growing and conflicting demands for both domestic consumption and industrial processing, more jackfruit needs to be grown in an organized manner, even if the research region has the ability to produce jackfruit for industrial processing. (Y.B. Byaruhanga *et al* ., 2019)

Production:

India is regarded as the jackfruit's motherland and is the world's second-largest producer. It is widely distributed throughout India, including the foothills of the Himalayas, Assam, Tripura, Bihar, Uttar Pradesh, and the southern Indian states of Kerala, Tamil Nadu, and Karnataka. In Indian agriculture and culture, jackfruit is important. In India, it was cultivated between 3000-6000 years ago. A common tree in Keralan homesteads, jackfruit is often grown as a shade crop on coffee plantations. In the eastern and southern regions of India, it is commonly referred to as "poor man's fruit." Ripe fruits are utilized as table fruits, while the tree's fragile fruits are used as vegetables. The traditional types only produce fruit once a year. Depending on the area and variety, blossoming often begins in mid-November and lasts until mid-February. Beginning in March and continuing through August, the sensitive fruits are available for purchase. June is when the fruits start to ripen. The late variety, though, can ripen in October. From November forward, it is typically impossible to find fresh and tender fruits. In India, commercial jackfruit cultivation is still in its infancy, mostly due to the challenge of obtaining high-quality planting materials. Jack is easily multiplied by seed. It takes 8–10 years for the seedlings to produce fruit. Obtaining true-to-type plants requires vegetative propagation because the crop is highly cross-pollinated. Among many other nutrients, jackfruit contains calcium, potassium, iron, sodium, zinc, thiamine, riboflavin, vitamin A, vitamin C, and niacin. Jackfruit is low in calories, with only 100 Jackfruit only has 94 calories per gram. Jackfruit has 303 mg of potassium per 100 g, making it a good source of the mineral. Foods high in potassium have been shown in studies to help decrease blood pressure. Vitamin C, an antioxidant that fortifies the immune system, shields the body from free radicals, and maintains healthy gums, is also abundant in jackfruit (Umesh *et al.,* 2010). Pureed jackfruit can be used as a base for cordials, juice, jam, jelly, and infant food.

Farming Methods:

Without extra care and farming methods, jack, one of the fruit crops, yields an abundance of fruits each year on farmlands and in secondary forest areas. As a result, they are automatically recognized as organic products. In addition to providing carbs and building muscle and strength, jackfruit is a wonderful source of several vitamins and minerals. Ripe jackfruit is thought to be both tasty and nourishing. It has a unique flavor and is sweet. Jack fruit has enormous potential for adding value. From the immature stage of jack fruit to the well-ripened stage, a vast array of products can be made. Every product has unique characteristics, such as taste, preference, and shelf life. Jackfruit's large size and weight make packing and transportation major obstacles to its effective marketing. Therefore, rather than the entire fruit, value-added goods are more relevant for commercial utility. Based on the most recent advancements in jackfruit processing, entrepreneurship has the potential to support a number of social and economic advancements, including the creation of jobs, revenue, and poverty alleviation, as well as enhancements to national food security, nutrition, and health. The economy will gain greatly from the expansion of this sector, which will lower post-harvest losses, provide jobs, and improve the lives of many people throughout the state, particularly those living in rural areas or agricultural catchments. (G. S. Chikkanna *et al*., 2021)

Due to their high pectin and cellulose content, jackfruit wastes—including the perianths of unfertilized fruits—have typically been processed to create syrups and jellies. Fruit rinds and other waste materials are used to make a nutritious feed for animals. In order to maximize digestion, it must be supplied. For improved digestibility, molasses-urea cake is therefore fed to calves combined with jackfruit waste. However, it only makes up roughly 16% of the fruit's overall width. As the fruit ripens, the amount of latex in the core increases, but it remains compact. As a source of vitamins, minerals, and calories, Artocarpus species contribute to the vital nutrition of people in every nation. The jackfruit has dietary value with a range of culinary applications. The tree's wood is used to make furniture and musical instruments. To prevent environmental problems, several activated carbons and colors are made from jackfruit peel. Utilizing jackfruit wastes properly can lower waste disposal costs while also increasing the jackfruit's economic worth. When deciding whether to grow jackfruit in certain regions, farmers and market vendors should provide information on consumer behavior about fresh fruit attributes generally. For a variety of industrial uses, the production of Artocarpus species such as cempedak and jackfruit are good sources of raw materials for the separation or extraction of color, carbons, fibers, and different carbohydrates like pectin, protein, starch, and cellulose, as well as their derivatives. (Antony Allwyn Sundarraj, Thottiam Vasudevan Ranganathan *et al*, 2018)

Jackfruit is the biggest fruit on the planet. India, Bangladesh, Thailand, Vietnam, Indonesia, and Nepal are the main producers of this fruit. A tree with many uses, jackfruit can be used for fruits, lumber, fodder, gum, dye, medicine, ornamental purposes, shade, shelterbelts, windbreaks, processed foods, veggies, and more. Jackfruits are monaecious, meaning that the male and female flowers are produced independently. Details on jackfruit, including its climatic requirements, varieties, propagation, processing, and marketing system, have been covered in this chapter. Indian varieties with crimson flesh have gained popularity recently. The most effective technique for propagating jackfruit is cleft grafting. In East and South East Asia, processed jackfruit is likewise becoming more and more popular. Jackfruit is used to make jam, jelly, juice, candies, dry chips, and more. (M. A. Rahim *et al.,* 2023)

Because of its edible fruits, Artocarpus heterophyllus Lam. is a fruit tree crop that is primarily produced in tropical areas. Despite being classified as an underused crop, jackfruit is becoming more and more popular in Uganda. The crop is under a lot of selective pressure due to rising demand, although the country's crop distribution and variety distribution are not documented. In order to establish a baseline for jackfruit production, a thriving market, and conservation, this study sought to identify the kinds and distribution of jackfruit in Uganda using traditional knowledge. 349 people participated in a cross-sectional survey that included 205 jackfruit traders and 144 jackfruit producers from three agro-ecological zones and three political areas. Direct observations and in-person interviews with a semi-structured questionnaire were used to gather data. Investigations were conducted into the classification of jackfruit kinds, the geographic location of the fruit's supply for traders, and the farmers' harvesting schedule. Through on-farm visits, the prevalence of types by household was ascertained. Descriptive, chi-square, and Cramer's V measure of association studies were among the data analytic methods used. The Central (46.0%) and Eastern (37.5%) political areas, the Southern and Eastern Lake Kyoga Basin (30.0%) agro-ecological zones, and Lake Victoria Crescent and Mbale Farmlands (41.1%) were the primary sources of jackfruit for traders. Four ethno-varieties of jackfruit were identified by classification based on fruit texture and pulp color: firm yellow (Kanaanansi), firm red (Namusaayi), firm white (Namata), and soft (Serebera). The agro-ecological zones and political regions with the lowest occurrences were Namata and Serebera. Jackfruit was collected by farmers all year round, with December and January being the busiest months. Baseline data for classifying jackfruit varieties came from folk knowledge. Namata and Serebera are under selection pressure to conserve their germplasm. Given that jackfruit grows well in a variety of climates, its production ought to be promoted in order to maintain food security and meet the growing demand. (Justine Nakintu, Eunice Olet, Morgan Andama Andama, Julius Lejju *et al.,* 2019)

Worldwide, jackfruit seeds are frequently disregarded and thrown away, which results in the underutilization of this priceless resource. By examining the availability of jackfruit, household-level seed usage and underuse, and the kinds of subsistence activities in the community, this study investigated the possibilities of using underutilized jackfruit seeds as an alternative source of human subsistence. As demonstrated by numerous international culinary traditions and current research findings, jackfruit seeds—which are sometimes disregarded—have enormous potential for use in both domestic and commercial settings. Through a variety of uses, most notably sustainable microbial fermentation and eco-friendly green extraction techniques that produce biochemicals and renewable energy sources, the importance of jackfruit seeds has been acknowledged globally. Jackfruit seeds' diverse applications not only highlight their economic worth but also add to the growing prospects in the sustainability conversation, particularly in the energy sector. The Portuguese word "jaca" is where the name "jackfruit" originates.

Jackfruit seeds are essential to traditional cuisines in places like Bangladesh, where they lend distinctive flavors to food and are used as a base for curries and stews. This has led to research into value addition and export possibilities. Similar to this, Brazilian researchers have discovered creative applications including fermenting, roasting, and turning seeds into flour, which provide farmers with a profitable substitute for cocoa. According to studies, Nigerians frequently roast, boil, or grind jackfruit seeds into flour to add to stews and soups as a source of protein. Additionally, these seeds are used to produce animal feed, which opens up new sources of income for agricultural economies. In line with customers' growing preference for vegetarian diets, jackfruit seeds have become popular in the US as a healthy meat alternative. As a result, customers may now select goods that reflect their values without sacrificing convenience or flavor. This pattern is indicative of a larger movement to satisfy a range of nutritional requirements with sustainably and ethically produced substitutes, such as those made from jackfruit seeds and the potential for multiple uses for jackfruit and its seeds.

Given the jackfruit's widespread use, particularly in India, its seeds have the potential to be used for a variety of reasons, including as a source of starch. This is demonstrated in a number of places where jackfruit seeds are roasted with salt and spices and then boiled or steamed to create delicious, healthful snacks. Similar to this, jackfruit seeds are traditionally used in Indian curries and gravies to add a unique texture and flavor to the dish. This creates a unique story for using jackfruit seeds in curries in various states. Numerous Indian businesspeople have been drawn to transform even more jackfruit seeds into flour as a result of the ongoing realization of this potential. They have also looked into using seeds as a gluten substitute in baking or as a thickening in other dishes. This helps to explain why pulverized jackfruit seeds are used as a paste and as a batter for dosas and idlis, which are thin pancakes (also called steamed rice cakes). This improves both their nutritional value and flavor. Pickling is another traditional method that is frequently used as a tangy and spicy side dish that improves the flavor of rice dishes. Jackfruit seeds, particularly boiled or roasted seeds, are important in vegetarian recipes since they are high in protein.(Chinchu Bose , Sabarinath ., 2024)

A variety of nutrients are abundant in jackfruit. It can serve as a source of comprehensive nourishment for customers. The fruit nearly has the exact nutrient equivalents of mother's, making it comparable to avocado and olives in terms of the healthier combination of nutrients for human dietary needs milk. It is a cheap and accessible addition to our main diet, high in proteins, iron, potassium, calcium, vitamin B and C, and carbohydrates. Its seeds are rich in proteins and can be relished as a nutritious nut. The practice of raising an agricultural commodity's economic worth and consumer appeal is known as value addition. Agricultural products can benefit from a variety of value-adding technologies, including processing and preservation, drying and dehydration, freezing technology, packing, labeling, and more. Jackfruit has a lot of potential for adding value. From the immature stage of jackfruit to the well-ripened stage, more than 100 dishes can be made. Every item has unique qualities, such as taste, preference, and shelf life. Growers and consumers are largely unaware of the significance of the fruit, seed, and rind. A significant amount of the jackfruit produced is wasted as a result of the growers' lack of coordinated marketing tactics. Utilizing the excess fruits that are available throughout the season and creating value-added goods are both crucial for enhancing farmers' livelihoods. The process of converting a product from its initial state to one that is more valuable is known as value addition. (Nazmun Naher, Forhad Hossain *et al* ., 2021)

An estimated $5.8 million worth of jackfruit is wasted annually from 0.4 to 0.5 million jackfruit trees in the Garo Hills as a result of inadequate infrastructure, a lack of scientific knowledge about processing and storage, and limited market access. In order to support the standardization of sustainable value addition practices for the area, the study intends to investigate the current state of jackfruit cultivation and utilization of locally available jackfruit as well as to document the value addition practices used by ethnic tribal communities in the Garo Hills of Meghalaya, India. The study was carried out in each of the Garo Hills' five districts. A basic random sample technique was used to choose two blocks from each district. Using the snowball sampling technique, 20 respondents were chosen from each block that was chosen, for a total of 200 respondents. Focused group discussions with the pertinent stakeholders were utilized to identify and document the ethnic value adding activities of tribal communities. Descriptive statistics and the Duncan Multiple Range Test were used to analyze the data. Due to the low percentage of respondents (30.5%) who used value-adding techniques and the insignificant marketing of raw jackfruit (3970 kg), the average waste percentage in Garo Hills was greater than half of the jackfruit production. The necessity for laboratory research to standardize these value addition processes in order to meet local and external market demands is evident from the identification, recording, and use study of ethnic value addition activities. (Sangma, Lahiri, Suresh *et al.,* 2023).

Functional values of jackfruit parts

Jackfruit is found all over in Bangladesh; but mainly in the month of Jaishtha and Ashar. It grows in plenty on the hilly areas of Chittagong and Sylhet and on the highland of Dhaka, Mymensingh, Comilla and Jessore. Beside these, it grows in India, Srilanka, Burma and Brazil. It has a rough and prickly skin.

Inside the skin the fruit is found to be composed of many juicy flakes. When it becomes ripe, it turns out to be delicious and succulent to eat. It is also a very nutritious fruit. Jackfruit seeds contain vitamin ''A'' and "C''. Various types of products can be prepared by jackfruit cell. Those with firmer, sweeter fruit are termed "varikkachakka," while those with less firmness and sweetness are called "koozhachakka." The immature fruit is known as polos in Sri Lanka and idichakka or idianchakka in Kerala. They are utilized in Sri Lankan, Andhranean, eastern Indian (Bengali), and Keralan cuisines in curry recipes that substitute spices for meat. Before the entire fruit can be sliced into edible pieces and prepared for consumption, the unripe jack fruit's skin must be peeled and thrown away. The young fruit is inedible when uncooked. Young jackfruit has a unique texture similar to fowl and a mild flavor. Cooked young jackfruit is used in the cuisines of India, Nepal, Bangladesh, Sri Lanka, Indonesia, Cambodia, Thailand, and Vietnam.

Ripe fruit seeds can be prepared by boiling them in salted water for approximately twenty-five minutes. They taste sweet and creamy. Roasted salted seed is also consumed and regarded as a delicacy in several regions of India. To get rid of the slimy component, seeds taken from completely ripe fruits are rinsed in water. To prevent them from drying out, seeds should be kept in closed plastic bags for a day or two right away. Soaking seeds for a full day in clean water improves germination. Plant seeds in a nursery bed with 70% soil and 30% organic matter, spaced 30 cm apart, for transplanting. To protect emerging seedlings, the seedbed should be slightly shielded from direct sunshine.

It might appear difficult to chop a jackfruit, but once it's open, the rest is simple and fun. From spring to summer, jackfruit is available in the market. A central pithy core and narrow ribbons of thin, but undeveloped, perianths make up 25–30% of the entire fruit, while the center of ripe fruit is composed of huge, sweet, yellow bulbs with a pleasant flavor (completely formed perianths). A smooth, round, light brown seed (endocarp) encased in a thin white membrane (exocarp) is found inside each bulb. The seed is 1.5 to 2.5 cm in thickness and 2-4 cm in length. A single fruit may contain 100–120 or even 500 seeds, making up 5–6% of the fruit overall. The color of the pump (bulb) can be bright orange, yellow, cream, or thin white. Fruit sizes vary greatly, ranging from tiny to large, and pulp thicknesses range from thin wafery to as thick as 0.5 cm. The pulp's flavor varies from somewhat insipid to extremely sweet, and its texture varies from soft to crisp. The pulp's flavor varies from very mild to heavily fragrant, and the entire fruit can be anywhere from 8 inches to 3 feet in size, with some weighing as much as 20 to 50 kg. Likewise, the tree's height falls between 50 and 60 feet.

A common vegetable, the soft jack fruit is used to make pickles and soup. Both ripe and unripe pulp are used to make chips and papads. The ripe fruit's luscious flesh can be consumed raw or preserved in syrup. Because it contains pectin, it can be used to make a variety of value-added goods, including jam and jelly. These processed goods have a sizable market in the United States, the United Kingdom, and the Gulf nations. The fruit's rind or skin and leaves make great livestock feed. The tree's golden, strong wood is prized for use in furniture construction. Additionally, jackfruit trees are planted to provide shade for cardamom, pepper, and betel plantations. (Morshada Khatun *et al.,* 2015)

In order to assess its potential use in foods, the physicochemical and functional characteristics of pectin (JFP), which was extracted from edible parts of raw jackfruit (an underutilized tropical fruit), including the pericarp and seed, at four distinct maturity stages (referred to as stages I, II, III, and IV), were described in terms of extraction yields, chemical composition, molecular weight, and antioxidant properties. (Cynthia Fontes-Candia *et al.,* 2023)

Vendors and the jackfruit processing business have thrown away the rinds and cores as garbage. It is estimated that over 60% of the entire jackfruit is wasted. The way these garbage are disposed of could harm the ecosystem. However, if apple waste is used properly, it may be made into a valuable commodity and garbage disposal costs can be decreased. Beneficial chemicals, such pectin, can be recovered from jackfruit wastes to lessen wastes and their detrimental effects on the environment. used alcohol precipitation and acid extraction to extract pectin from jackfruit rind. optimized the extraction process for the yield and purity of jackfruit waste pectin by using various extraction (acid and chelating agent) and precipitation (alcohol and acetone) medium. Low temperature oven drying was found to be advantageous in each of these situations for producing high-quality pectin powder. The morphology and surface appearance of commercial and analytical grade pectin powder, as well as the jackfruit waste pectin powder modified by drying techniques, were displayed by SEM. Here are the micrographs. According to the micrographs, every pectin particle had a rough surface and an uneven granular powder shape. Rough and uneven surfaces were also discovered in a prior investigation on mango and apple pomace pectin. Indistinct particles and clots were visible in a picture of spray-dried pectin. The aggregation of pectin and the poor particle size of the spray-dried powder could be the cause of this. Because of its small particle size, commercial pectin also produced comparable results.

Jackfruit waste pectin produced by freeze-drying, spray-drying, vacuum-oven-drying, oven-drying, analytical-grade, and commercial-grade pectin samples showed infrared (diffuse reflectance FTIR) spectra (400–4000 cm). The conformation of pectin bands in the standard region, typically between 1000 and 2000 cm, for the principal chemical and functional groups was evaluated using FTIR analysis. The esterified and free carboxyl groups were indicated by bands at around 1750 cm−Citation1 and 1650 cm−Citation1, respectively. As the DE values rose, it was found that the esterified carboxyl groups exhibited a growing tendency in their intensities and band areas. The present study's FTIR spectra revealed no significant structural variations among the pectin samples made using different drying methods. The pectin structures of jackfruit waste were similar to those of food-grade and analytical pectin samples. The stretching vibrations of the (C–OH) side groups and the (C–O–C) glycosidic bond vibration are represented by the area in the figure between 1000 and 1140 cm. (Begum, Rokeya *et al.,* 2017)

The versatile and underappreciated jackfruit (Artocarpus heterophyllus) has enormous potential in the food, pharmaceutical, nutraceutical, and other industries. Minerals including calcium, magnesium, potassium, phosphorus, iron, and zinc, as well as vital nutrients like vitamins, dietary fiber, and carbs, are abundant in this fruit. Jackfruit seeds include bioactive substances such flavonoids, saponins, and isoflavones that have anti-cancer and health-promoting qualities, as well as lectins that have antibacterial qualities. Although they are sometimes disregarded, jackfruit seeds have several health advantages, such as improving digestion, having anti-aging and anti-carcinogenic qualities, and creating an environment that is conducive to good gut flora. Jackfruit seeds, which make up more than 15% of the fruit's weight, are a useful byproduct that may find use in a number of different industries. In addition to being a thickening and binding agent, jackfruit seed flour possesses potent antioxidant qualities. Jackfruit seed particles at the nanoscale have improved antimicrobial qualities, which increases their industrial uses. This review offers thorough information on how jackfruit seeds are processed into a variety of value-added products, their potential medical uses, and the physicochemical changes that occur throughout various processing techniques like drying, fermentation, and extraction. Furthermore, the seeds support immune system evaluation, bone health, and free radical defense. Given jackfruit seeds' substantial nutritional and commercial potential, it is critical to encourage their use in order to reduce fruit peel waste and improve nutritional security. Jackfruit seeds are normally light brown and spherical in shape, measuring 2 cm to 3 cm in length and 1 cm to 1.5 cm in diameter. They are wrapped by a fragile whitish membrane. When stored in a cool, humid atmosphere, these seeds can last up to a month. They include easily absorbed proteins, carbs (40-50%), minerals, vitamins, and phytonutrients such as isoflavones, lignans, and saponins, which may provide health benefits. A single jackfruit tree can produce 390 kilogram of seeds annually.

Jackfruit seeds are already being used to generate a variety of culinary products, with promising results. Only a few review papers have been published on this issue, focusing on the physicochemical properties, bioactive components, antioxidant capacity, microstructure, and value of jackfruit seed flour in baking and extruded items. Potential uses for jackfruit seed and jackfruit seed starch in the food and associated industries. However, this review provides a contemporary and comprehensive understanding of the use of jackfruit seeds by combining studies from nutrition, functioning, and industrial applications. The evaluation focuses on the sustainable use of jackfruit seeds, emphasizing their ability to reduce agricultural waste and assist circular economy activities while also supporting environmental sustainability. Jackfruit seeds have already been employed to make a range of culinary dishes, with promising results. Only a few review papers have been published on this topic, with an emphasis on the physicochemical properties, bioactive components, antioxidant capacity, microstructure, and value of jackfruit seed flour in baking and extruded products. Jackfruit seed and jackfruit seed starch have potential applications in food and related sectors. However, this review gives a current and thorough understanding of the usage of jackfruit seeds by merging studies on nutrition, function, and industrial applications. The review focuses on the sustainable use of jackfruit seeds, emphasizing their ability to reduce agricultural waste and contribute to circular economy activities while also supporting environmental sustainability. (Mohammed Fabil · Praveen Kumar Dubey *et al.,* 2024)

Jackfruit seeds, often dismissed as by-products, are a powerhouse of nutrients and bioactive compounds. This comprehensive review explores various aspects of jackfruit seeds, including their nutritional composition, bioactive compounds, and health-promoting properties. Jackfruit seeds are a rich source of starch (12.86–17.90 g/100 g), protein (18%), fiber (1.56–3.92 g/100 g), minerals, and bioactive compounds such as phenolics, flavonoids, and saponins. These bioactive compounds have been found to protect against oxidative stress-related diseases. Moreover, jackfruit seeds demonstrate promising health effects, including antidiabetic, anticancer, hepatoprotective, and antimicrobial properties. Incorporating jackfruit seed flour into bread items boosts their nutritional profiles and functional qualities, such as high oil and water absorption capacity. Understanding the nutritional profile, health benefits, and functional properties of jackfruit seeds is critical. This understanding provides as a foundation for developing bakery food items with enhanced nutritional profiles and possible health advantages, which may be of substantial importance to the food industry.(Julieta Melissa López-Martínez, Imran Ahmad *et al.,* 2024)

Jackfruit is a little-known and underutilized crop that has the potential to be used in human diet. This study used multivariate data analysis to assess the effect of ripening stages on the physicochemical, carbohydrate content, and antioxidant properties of jackfruit seed flour. Fruit matures with lower protein (18.56% to 12.15%) and ash content (3.80% to 2.63%), but higher dietary fiber, carbohydrate, and functional characteristics. Jackfruit seed flour contains inositol, sorbitol, glucose, fructose, sucrose, maltose, and raffinose, with glucose, fructose, and raffinose increasing with maturity, with the exception of sucrose and maltose. To study the similarities and differences between cultivars and maturity stages, the main component analysis was performed on four cultivars and their maturity stages in many characteristics such as physicochemical, functional qualities, and antioxidant activity. The current study found that flour can be useful in the manufacture of value-added food products. (Radha Kushwaha, Neha Taslim Fatima, Monika Singh, Vinti Singh, Seeratpreet Kaur *et al.,* 2020)

The current study intends to create novel goods with improved functional features (expansion ratio, bulk density, and antioxidant properties) using jackfruit seed flour and soy flour, both of which are becoming more widely available in India. Soy flour extrusion was standardized based on product reaction, resulting in the best expansion ratio, lowest bulk density, and maximum in-vitro antioxidant characteristics. The optimized parameters were then used to make extrudates from composite blends of Jackfruit seed flour and soy flour at varying percentages ranging from 20 to 80%. Prior to extrusion, a fraction of equilibrated composite blends of soy and jackfruit seed flour were analyzed for functional and antioxidant characteristics. The total flavonoid concentration was found to be somewhat greater in post-extruded samples. In-vitro antioxidant activities were much higher, with only a minor improvement in antioxidant characteristics after extrusion. HPLC analysis of the products revealed the presence of phenolic compounds such as ascorbic acid, gallic acid, and vanillin, as well as flavonoids such as catechin and daidzein. Texture study revealed that the extrudates' hardness was satisfactory. Post-extrusion study of the newly produced product revealed higher functional values than the control mix comprising simply soy flour. As a result of the investigation, it was determined that the addition of jackfruit seed flour improved the overall functional properties of extruded products. (Chakraborty P, Bhattacharyya DK, Ghosh *et al.,* 2022)

Jackfruit seeds are a highly nutritious, underutilized byproduct that can help fight malnutrition and promote a healthy lifestyle. This paper looks at the nutritional, physiological, and physical aspects of jackfruit seed flour (JSF) and how it affects extrusion and baking. A thorough investigation revealed that JSF in extruded and baked products enhances nutritional characteristics and increases functional properties such as bulk density and water holding capacity, while decreasing oil holding capacity and expansion ratio. Furthermore, the absence of gluten reduced the texture and color qualities of JSF at greater concentrations. Consumer research found that extruded items incorporating JSF were more acceptable than baking products with equivalent substitutes. However, suitable formulations are required to balance nutritional enhancement with desired textural features, and the long-term use of this waste can result in the development of a wide range of nutritious food products. (Shibil Mohammed, Praveen Kumar Dubey *et al .,* 2024)

Jack fruit is a heterozygous and cross-pollinated crop, leading to significant variety in production, size, shape, and quality of fruit, as well as maturity duration. Cutting jackfruit may look difficult, but once opened, it's simple and delightful. Jackfruit is typically available in the market from spring until summer. The plant has enormous, flavorful yellow sweet bulbs (completely grown perianths) surrounded by thin, undeveloped perianths and a center pith. Core accounts around 25-30% of the whole fruit. Each bulb contains a smooth, round, light brown seed (endocarp) surrounded by a thin white membrane (exocarp). The seed measures 2-4 cm long and 1.5–2.5 cm thick. A single fruit might contain 100-120 or even 500 seeds, accounting for 5-6 percent of the entire weight. The pump (bulb) colors range from thin white, cream, yellow, and vivid orange. Fruit sizes range from small to large, with pulp thickness ranging from thin wafery to 0.5 cm. Sweetness ranges from slightly insipid to highly sweet, and pulp texture varies from soft to crunchy. The pulp flavor varies from moderate to intense, and the fruit size can range from 8 inches to 3 feet, with some weighing up to 50 kg. The tree height ranges from 50 to 60 feet.

Tender jackfruit is a popular vegetable used to make soup and pickles. Chips and papads are made from both ripe and unripe pulp. The luscious pulp of the ripe fruit, It can be consumed fresh or preserved in syrup, and its pectin content makes it suitable for making jam and jelly, as well as a variety of other value-added products. These processed items have a good market in the United States, United Kingdom, and Gulf countries. Cattle can benefit greatly from the rind and leaves of the fruit. The golden firm wood of the tree is valuable for building furniture. Jackfruit trees are grown to provide shade to betel, pepper, and cardamom plants. The seeds, which have similar compositions to grains, can be consumed boiled or roasted and utilized in various culinary recipes. Jack fruit is very seasonal, and the seeds have a short shelf life, leading to waste during the excess. Seed flour is a versatile product that may be used for value-adding and blending with other grains without compromising the final product's functionality or sensory profile.

Incorporating seed flour into deep fat fried goods significantly reduces fat absorption. The ripening fruit is fibrous and contains carbohydrates such as glucose, fructose, xylose, rhamnose, arabinose, and galactose. Seeds contain high levels of carbs, proteins, fiber, and B-complex vitamins. The Chinese believe that jackfruit pulp and seeds might help them overcome the effects of drinking. In India, jack seed is commonly used as an antidote for heavy drinkers. Resin found in the bark's latex is occasionally used to seal gaps in earthen vats and other items. The leaves' latex has the ability to eradicate germs. The main protein found in jack seeds, jacalin, has shown promise as a tool for assessing the immunological state of HIV-positive patients (Morton, 1987). As an excellent source of vitamin A, vitamin C, and pectin, jackfruit also aids in blood purification and the relief of pancreatic disorders. With all of these therapeutic benefits and effective components in value-added products, there is still more room for using seed flour in convenience foods to increase marketability and generate economic employment for rural women. (Shadab Butool, Masrath Butool *et al.,* 2015)

One strategy to fight hunger is to take advantage of underutilized local resources that are abundant in nutrients and bioactive substances. In many parts of the world, jackfruit seeds are eaten after being treated to enhance their biological and nutritional qualities. By identifying the optimal treatment or treatments to produce jackfruit seed flours with good nutritional qualities, the current study sought to aid in the fight against malnutrition. Jackfruit seeds were thus separated into four batches, with the first batch serving as the control (untreated) and the others being roasted, blanched, soaked, and cooked, in that order. Both the functional and chemical characteristics were evaluated. The findings demonstrated that while the carbohydrate content (79.90 to 80.42%) increased, the protein content (18.11 to 15.93%), lipid content (1.81 to 1.15%), and overall anti-nutrient content decreased significantly ($p < 0.05$) as a result of the treatments. The ethanolic extract's phenol and flavonoid contents rose dramatically ($p < 0.05$) as a result of the treatments. Blanched seeds had the highest antioxidant activity when it came to capturing 2,2-diphenyl-1-picrylhydrazyl (DPPH). Cooking and soaking together have demonstrated a greater capacity to absorb water and oil (24.20% and 23.20%, respectively). The best methods for producing flour with more potentially health-promoting ingredients were blanching, soaking, and cooking. (Donald Sévérin Dangang Bossi, Saint-Victorien Ganota, Stéphano Tambo Téné, Marc Bertrand Dandji Saah et al .,2024)

A common household fruit in tropical regions is jackfruit. The fruit's nutritious value is the main reason it is considered Kerala's state fruit. Despite the fruit's enormous potential for use, the primary obstacle to its full potential is the produce's unavailability during the off-season. One of the most neglected parts of jackfruit is its seed. Another problem is the market's dearth of ready-to-use forms. In light of the current problems, a study was carried out to prepare jackfruit seed for use. Vacuum packing was employed for the study, taking into consideration the cost of the packaging as well as additional advantages. To increase the jackfruit seed's shelf life, a variety of packing materials, including LDPE 500 G, LDPE 400 G, PP 260 G, and HDPE 180 G, were investigated. Taking into account the properties of packaging, the study supported the use of PP 260 as packing material. Additionally, a comparison of the powdered jackfruit seeds processed by dry and wet methods was conducted. The analysis revealed that there was no discernible difference in the seed powder's characteristics. The dry process approach is widely accepted, despite the tedious nature of the process (Aarcha Vallath, Amrutha, K. P, Basil, M, Harikrishnan, M. George Mathew et al 2019).

Jack fruit seed protein

Jackfruit is made up of a number of berries with brown seeds and yellow pulp that are protected by a hard shell. These fruits have an oblong-cylindric shape and are usually between 30 and 40 cm long, though they can occasionally reach 90 cm. Although a weight of 25 kg has been recorded, the fruit typically weighs between 3.5 and 10 kg. After being processed, jackfruit leftovers can make up as much as 70% of the fruit's weight. The seeds, which can make up 8% to 15% of the fruit's weight, are one type of such residue.Jackfruit seeds are a good source of dietary fiber (3.19%) and carbohydrate (22%). Furthermore, the phytonutrients lignans, isoflavones, and saponins found in jackfruit seeds have a variety of health advantages, including anticancer, antihypertensive, antiaging, antioxidant, and antiulcer properties. Another ingredient found in jackfruit seeds is protein, which can range from 17.8% to 37% of the seed depending on the kind. (Swami *et al.,* Citation2012).
The characterization of characteristics like water/oil absorption, solubility, jellification, emulsifying capacity, and foaming capacity is technologically significant because they dictate the possible use of protein isolate food ingredients. As a result, jackfruit seeds may be a potential source of a protein isolate. (Bernardino-Nicanor *et al.,* Citation2014).

Jackfruit seed protein concentrate (JSPC) is made by alkaline solubilization with the aid of ultrasonography and isoelectric precipitation. A hydrolysate (JSPH) containing pancreatin is obtained, the amino acid profile is determined, and the techno-functional characteristics and antioxidant capacity are assessed. At three hours, the maximum level of hydrolysis (18.87%) was achieved. The JSPC and JSPH were shown to contain seven essential amino acids: valine, leucine, isoleucine, methionine, threonine, phenylalanine, and lysine. Alanine, glycine, proline, serine, aspartic acid, glutamic acid, tyrosine, and hydroxyproline were the additional amino acids that were found. As the pH deviated from the isoelectric pH of 4.0 (pI ~ 4.0), the solubility, foaming, and emulsifying capacity for both improved in terms of the techno-functional qualities. JSPH had a greater antioxidant capacity (95.56%) than JSPC (56.37%). Finally, a protein hydrolysate and concentrate was produced having techno-functional qualities that might be applied to food compositions as emulsions and additives. (Dulce María de Jesús Miss-Zacarías, Montserrat Calderón-Santoyo *et al.,*2024)

Generally Recognized As Safe (GRAS), five filamentous fungi, including Penicillium expansum, Aspergillus niger, Aspergillus oryzae, Rhizopus microsporus, and Candida intermedia, were used in the bioconversion of jackfruit seed into a valuable product like Single-Cell Protein (SCP) through submerged fermentation. Fungal biomass and SCP synthesis were increased when jackfruit seed extracts were supplemented with inorganic nitrogen sources and glucose as a carbon source. On the ninth day of fermentation, A. niger produced the highest biomass and protein production of all the different fungal strains, weighing 4.01 ± 0.07 g/l and 1.82 ± 0.03 g/l, respectively. P. expansum came in second with 3.65 ± 0.04 g/l and 1.68 ± 0.03 g/l, respectively. Growth of C. intermedia was not observed in all experimental medium. The fungal biomass has demonstrated low levels of crude fiber, crude fat, and and the overall amount of genomic DNA varied between 1.10 ± 0.20 and 4.95 ± 0.40%. In sugar supplementation media, A. niger and P. expansum were the most effective in converting sugar to biomass (55.83 ± 0.3% and 54.71 ± 0.4%, respectively). The most promising fungal strains for producing fungal biomass protein from low-cost agro-waste material were P. expansum and A. niger. (Ankita Chakraborty & Jayati Bhowal *et al.,* 2023)

One important source of nutrition, especially protein, is jackfruit seeds. According to studies, there are roughly 9.9 to 10.2 grams of protein in 100 grams of jackfruit seeds. They are a useful supplement to many diets because of their high protein content. It has been demonstrated that adding jackfruit seed flour to baked foods improves their nutritional profile. For example, when 10 grams of jackfruit seed flour were added to 100 grams of wheat flour in chocolate cake recipes, the amount of protein and ash increased but the amount of fat decreased. (Papori Bora, Pranati Das and Mridula Saikia Barooah *et al.,* 2018)

It's crucial to remember that jackfruit seeds include antinutritional elements that can impact nutrient absorption, including tannins, phytates, and trypsin inhibitors. Roasting and germination are two processing techniques that might lessen these antinutrients, making the seeds safer and more palatable.(Sherrin Royees and Dr. Pragya Pandey *et al.,* 2022)

The protein content of jackfruit seeds varies by species and processing technique, ranging from 7 to 10 grams per 100 grams. Leucine and valine, two important amino acids that are good for muscle growth and repair, are part of their amino acid composition.(Ullah, R. *et al.* 2017).

Animal growth depressions, poor feed digestibility, and even death have been linked to anti-nutritional substances found in jackfruit seeds. The nutritional content of the jackfruit seed meal has been increased as a result of the employment of various processing methods, including as chemical detoxification, boiling, roasting, fermentation, soaking in plain water, or combinations of two or more treatments, to eliminate these anti-nutrients. (Noor *et al.,* 2021).

Because fermentation breaks down complicated protein structures into simpler amino acids, which are easier to absorb, it can boost the bioavailability of proteins. In comparison to raw seeds, fermentation increased the protein content of fermented jackfruit seed meals, according to a study analyzing their chemical makeup.(O. O. Effiong, V. N. Ebegbulem , N. P. Jimmy *et al.,* 2024)

Made up of amino acids, proteins are macromolecules that function as building blocks, sustain structure, and act as hormones, enzymes, and biochemical catalysts in the body. The prevalence of underweight and stunted growth in children, as well as insufficient protein defects, might result from dietary protein deficiencies. These seeds are a great source of food nutrients and high in protein and carbs. On a dry basis, the protein content of jackfruit seeds can reach 7.04%, whereas the protein content of seed flour can reach 16.01%. Therefore, jackfruit seeds may be a viable new plant protein and mineral source. (Md Akram Hossain, Md. Forshed Dewan, Mir Tuhin Billah, *et al.,*2023).

If properly prepared, jackfruit seeds can be a good source of protein. The protein fraction from jackfruit seeds can be used in food compositions to help meet the demand for protein. Gaining knowledge of the physicochemical and functional characteristics of dried and isolated proteins helps to better understand their hydrothermal behavior. The usage of isolated proteins as a component in the creation of foods enhanced with protein is growing. Knowing an isolated protein's physicochemical and functional characteristics beforehand makes it easier to incorporate it into new food formulations. Proteins should ideally have a number of desirable functional qualities, including as solubility, water-holding capacity, gel forming ability, and foaming capacity, for improved use as an ingredient. A protein's increased solubility raises Protein's capacity to froth and form emulsions improves meal structure and increases protein digestibility. (M. Amdadul Haque, Fatema Akter, Habibur Rahman, M. A. Baqui *et al.,* 2020).

Jackfruit seed starch has a darker color than Purity 4 starch but a lighter color than Novation 2300 starch. When compared to modified starches, the jackfruit seed starch needed less gelatinization energy and had a smaller gelatinization temperature range than Purity 4. Compared to commercially modified starches, jackfruit seed starch had a lower peak viscosity. Similarly, the solubility, swelling power, and setback viscosity of jackfruit seed starch displayed comparable patterns. According to the study's findings, jackfruit seed natural starch may be utilized in place of modified starches in systems that require starch with high mechanical and/or thermal shear stability. (Amornrat Mukprasirt, Kamontip Sajjaanantakul *et al.,* 2024)

Jackfruit seeds for human consumption. The seeds include phytonutrients such lignans, saponins, and isoflavones that are good for human health. Up to a certain point, the addition of jackfruit seed flour to deep-fried foods reduces the absorption of fat. The seeds' high fiber content helps avoid constipation, lessen the risk of heart disease, and aid in weight loss. They are also a good source of dietary fiber and B-complex vitamins. Additionally, resistant starch found in jackfruit seeds regulates blood sugar and maintains gut health. According to Maurya and Mogra, jackfruit seeds have antimicrobial properties that help prevent foodborne illnesses. Additionally, the seeds contain a crucial lectin called jacalin, which is used as a method to assess the immune system of an individual with HIV. In India, the seeds are an essential part of an antidote made for heavy drinkers, and in China, they are known to help overcome the toxicity caused by alcohol.

The seeds are rich in magnesium, which is essential for decreasing blood pressure and preserving bone health since it facilitates the absorption of calcium, which strengthens bones. The seeds' high content of highly soluble protein also helps to prevent and alleviate anxiety and mental stress. Because of their low capacity to absorb fat and water, the seeds can help prevent obesity.The seeds are rich in magnesium, which is essential for decreasing blood pressure and preserving bone health since it facilitates the absorption of calcium, which strengthens bones. The seeds' high content of highly soluble protein also helps to prevent and alleviate anxiety and mental stress. Because of their low capacity to absorb fat and water, the seeds can help prevent obesity. (Braz. J *et al.,* 2019)

Numerous minerals, lignans, isoflavones, saponins, and phytonutrients are also included in jackfruit seeds. As a result, jackfruit seeds are a common ingredient in many recipes. The smooth surface and bell-shaped jackfruit seed starch (JFSS) granules range in size from 5 to 10 μm. According to Rengsutthi and Charoenrein, JFSS has a lot of potential in the food sector, particularly for usage as a thickener, stabilizer, and binding agent. (Phuong Lan Tran, Dang Hai Dang Nguyen *et al.,* 2015)

A tetrameric two-chain lectin with a molecular mass of 65 kDa, jacalin is the main protein found in jackfruit (Artocarpus heterophyllus) seeds. It consists of a light β chain with 20–21 amino acid residues and a heavy α chain with 133 amino acid residues. Even in its sialylated form, it exhibits great specificity for the α-O-glycoside of the disaccharide Thomsen–Friedenreich antigen (Galβ1–3GalNAc). Because of this characteristic, jacalin can be used to examine a variety of O-linked glycoproteins, especially human IgA1. Jacalin is a unique substance that is highly mitogenic for human CD4+ T cells, which makes it a valuable tool for assessing the immunological status of clients with HIV-1 infection. Jacalin is a desirable and affordable lectin due to its abundance of source material, ease of purification, yield, and stability. It has been used in a variety of fields, including the examination of O-linked glycoproteins, the identification of tumors, the investigation of IgA-nephropathy, and the extraction of human plasma glycoproteins (IgA1, C1-inhibitor, hemopexin, and α2-HSG). (S Kabir *et al.,*2020).

Reverse micelles' ability to extract protein from jackfruit seed flour was assessed. Water, butanol as a solvent, and sodium dodecyl sulfate (SDS) as a surfactant made up the reverse micelle system. Batch systems were used to examine the effects of temperature, molar ratio H2O SDS-1, butanol concentration (mass %), stirring time, and flour mass. The only concentration that offered ideal extraction conditions, according to the adjusted linear regression model, was butanol (41.16%). The optimal extraction yield was achieved at 25°C, 120 minutes of stirring time, 100 mg of flour mass, and a ratio of H2O SDS-1 of 50, according to the surface response study. According to experimental findings, an extraction yield of 79.00% was achievable.(Rafael da Costa Ilhéu Fontan *et al.,* 2019 **)**

As customer demand for plant-based proteins rises, food manufacturers are vying for new plant proteins with specific properties. The purpose of this study is to separate the protein fraction from jackfruit seeds and evaluate the physicochemical and functional characteristics of the protein powder. The protein content of the seeds was extracted using centrifugation and pH treatments, and the concentrate was then turned into powder using a spray drying technique. The jackfruit seeds protein isolate (JSPI) was examined for its physicochemical characteristics, including crystallinity, morphology, and particle size distribution, as well as its functional characteristics, including solubility, gelling capacity, and emulsion qualities. Fourier-transform infrared (FTIR) spectroscopy was also used to identify the secondary structural components of JSPI. It was estimated that the prepared JSPI had roughly 76.89% protein Solubility in an aquatic solvent: 78.44%. In a salt solution, the lowest JSPI gelation concentration was 12%. The solvent's pH had a major impact on the foaming and emulsifying qualities. Nearly 75% of the particles in the protein isolate fell within a same size distribution range, and it had a moderate bulk density and an amorphous shape. The β-sheet has the largest content (50.28%), making it the dominating secondary structural element, according to the conformational research. The JSPI appears to have adequate functional and physicochemical properties for usage in protein-enriched meals, based on the qualities that have been identified. (M. Amdadul Haque, Fatema Akter, Habibur Rahman, M. A. Baqui *et al.,* 2020)

One possible element in food formulation is jackfruit seed flour. It has potential uses in the food business. According to earlier studies, jackfruit seed flour has a high bulk density and water absorption capability, making it suitable for use as a thickening and binding agent used in baking. The results of several investigations have demonstrated that the roasting temperature and duration have an impact on the functional qualities of jackfruit seed flour. The acceptability of jackfruit seed flour for use in food manufacturing is determined by its functional qualities, which include bulk density, water solubility index, oil absorption capacity, water absorption capacity, foam capacity, and foam stability.

The intricate relationship between physicochemical, molecular conformation, composition, and structure is represented by functional characteristics of food ingredients, along with the characteristics of the setting in which they are evaluated and connected. The physical and chemical characteristics of proteins that affect how they behave in food systems during preparation, processing, storage, and consumption are known as functional properties. These characteristics also affect the organoleptic qualities and quality of food systems. The fundamental functional characteristics that demonstrate the structural behavior of flour in food systems are its ability to absorb water, oil, gel, foam, and emulsify. In food processing, the functional qualities of jackfruit seed flour are essential for creating novel goods. The physical qualities of baked goods, such as their softness and swelling, are greatly influenced by the high water absorption capacity and good foaming qualities of raw jackfruit seed flour. Raw jackfruit seed flour's high oil absorption capacity demonstrated its good flavor retention rate and potential for use in food systems such ground meat compositions. Studies have shown that roasting jackfruit seeds affects the flour's functional qualities, including its capacity to absorb water, its bulk density, and its ability to produce foam. It results in the expansion of crude fiber and the gelatinization of carbohydrates, which raises the body's ability to absorb water of jack fruit seed flour. (Abidin M.Z., Malik N.H. , Abdullah N *et al.,* 2024)

Jackfruit seeds are a valuable, sustainable, and underutilized source of plant protein. They offer a rich amino acid profile, antioxidant benefits, and functional food applications. By incorporating them into diets through flour, protein isolates, or whole seed preparations, they can serve as an affordable and eco-friendly protein source. Jackfruit seeds contain 13.50% to 16.01% protein by weight in their raw or flour form, making them a moderate source of plant-based protein. However, protein isolates extracted from jackfruit seeds can reach up to 68.29% purity, comparable to common legume-based protein sources. Jackfruit seed protein contains essential amino acids required for human health, including: Histidine – Important for tissue repair and growth. Threonine – Supports digestive and immune function, Valine, Isoleucine, and Leucine – Branched-chain amino acids (BCAAs) that aid muscle development. However, methionine and tryptophan are found in lower quantities, meaning jackfruit seeds should be consumed alongside complementary protein sources like legumes or grains for a balanced amino acid intake. Studies also show that the polypeptide composition of jackfruit seed protein ranges from 17 to 26 kDa, with β-sheet and random coil structures contributing to its functional properties. Jackfruit seed protein is beneficial due to its antioxidant properties, digestive benefits, and role in muscle maintenance. Jackfruit seeds contain phenolic compounds, which help neutralize free radicals and reduce oxidative stress. The protein hydrolysates from jackfruit seeds have shown potential in lowering inflammation and improving metabolic health. Jackfruit seed protein contains resistant starch, which promotes gut health by acting as a prebiotic.It reduces the glycemic response, making it beneficial for people with diabetes. Due to its high lysine and leucine content, jackfruit seed protein can aid in muscle recovery and tissue repair. It can be an alternative protein source for vegetarians and vegans. (Dulce María de Jesús Miss-Zacarías, *et al.,* 2024)

Jackfruit is extensively grown in India, neighboring countries, and parts of Africa. After consuming the edible portion of the ripe fruit, the seeds—rich in carbohydrates and proteins—are often discarded as waste. This study aimed to examine the functional properties of raw and blended jackfruit seed flours to explore their potential use alongside wheat flour in various food formulations. Findings indicated that while lye-peeled seeds had lower nutrient content, they were preferred for their color and flavor. The research highlighted the significant potential of jackfruit seed flour in food applications. Factors influencing the functional properties of both raw and blended flours were analyzed. Due to their high water and oil absorption capacities, as well as other beneficial properties, these flour blends can be effectively utilized in bakery products, as protein supplements, and as functional ingredients in food processing. (Chowdhury A roy, Bhattacharyya *et al.,* 2012)

Regarding the amino acids and chemical makeup of the jackfruit seed, there were differences among all the treatments flour. According to protein content, essential amino acids, dietary fibre, and vitamin C content, thermal jackfruit seed flour produced the greatest results. Essential amino acid-containing plant-based protein flour is a key component in relation to the functional ingredient's end-use characteristics. To maximize its health advantages for future uses, more research on the toxicity and antinutritional component in jackfruit seeds is required. The chemical composition of jackfruit seed flour is also impacted by the processing method. When compared to raw jackfruit seed flour, the protein content of thermal jackfruit seed flour increased by the greatest amount (61%). Protein denaturation, which is followed by the aggregation of either soluble or insoluble complexes of proteins, may be the cause of the increase in protein content that occurs when jackfruit seeds are heated. Protein extraction from plants essentially consists of an extraction step and protein precipitation, which can be achieved via flocculation, autocoagulation (fermentation), thermocoagulation (temperature action), ultrafiltration, and extraction using organic solvents. The highest necessary amino acid content was found in jackfruit seed flour, which was followed by raw and germinated jackfruit seeds. Leucine was the most prevalent amino acid in thermal jackfruit seed flour, whereas lysine and phenylalanine were the most abundant amino acids in jackfruit seed flour that had germinated. Histidine, threonine, valine, isoleucine, and leucine levels were all raised by thermal jackfruit seed flour. The thermal jackfruit seed flour samples had the lowest levels of ash, crude fat, carbohydrates, and total dietary fibre out of the three samples, according to proximate analysis. The maximum protein content (24.94%) was found in heated jackfruit seed flour, but the highest vitamin C content (78.78 mg/100 g) was found in germinated jackfruit seed flour. Three distinct treatments' flour compositions revealed that the while heated jackfruit seed flour had a much higher energy value, germinated jackfruit seed flour had the highest starch content. In summary, heated jackfruit seed flour has a high protein and dietary fiber content in addition to vitamin C. (Zuwariah, I., Noor Fadilah, M.B., Hadijah, H. and Rodhiah, R. *et al.,* 2018)

Inositol, sorbitol, glucose, fructose, sucrose, maltose, and raffinose are all present in jackfruit seed flour; of these, glucose, fructose, sucrose, and raffinose, among others, increased with maturation, with the exception of sucrose and maltose. To examine the similarities and differences between cultivars and maturity stages, principal component analysis was performed on four cultivars and their stages of maturity in a variety of areas, including physicochemical, functional, and antioxidant activities. The current study's findings demonstrated the potential utility of flour in the creation of food items with added value. (Radha Kushwaha, Neha Taslim Fatima, Monika Singh, Vinti Singh*, et al.,* 2020).

Value Addition in Jack fruit seeds

Jackfruit seeds include bioactive substances such flavonoids, saponins, and isoflavones that have anti-cancer and health-promoting qualities, as well as lectins that have antibacterial qualities. Although they are sometimes disregarded, jackfruit seeds have several health advantages, such as improving digestion, having anti-aging and anti-carcinogenic qualities, and creating an environment that is conducive to good gut flora. Jackfruit seeds, which make up more than 15% of the fruit's weight, are a useful byproduct that may find use in a number of different industries. In addition to being a thickening and binding agent, jackfruit seed flour possesses potent antioxidant qualities. Jackfruit seed particles at the nanoscale have improved antimicrobial qualities, which increases their industrial uses. This review offers thorough information on how jackfruit seeds are processed into a variety of value-added products, their potential medical uses, and the physicochemical changes that occur throughout various processing techniques like drying, fermentation, and extraction. Furthermore, the seeds support immune system evaluation, bone health, and free radical defense. Given jackfruit seeds' substantial nutritional and commercial potential, it is critical to encourage their use in order to reduce fruit peel waste and improve nutritional security. Additionally, by highlighting an underutilized resource, this research offers a fresh viewpoint on the all-encompassing use of jackfruit seeds, highlighting their contribution to lowering food waste and promoting environmental sustainability.

A significant public health concern today is the prevalence of lifestyle diseases including cancer, diabetes, and cardiovascular disease around the world. Natural resource depletion and environmental damage have resulted from unsustainable farming practices brought on by the growing global population and the need for increased food supply. The modern Asian-Indian diet is higher in refined carbohydrates and lower in proteins than other dietary patterns. Growing awareness of the link between diet and disease has led to a rise in the trend of mixing various underused and more nutrient-dense flours with wheat flour. Because of their potential to correct nutritional deficiencies, lower the risk of disease, and support sustainable food systems, research into underused resources like jackfruit seeds has attracted a lot of attention. Usually spherical and light brown, jackfruit seeds have a delicate white membrane enclosing them. They measure roughly 2 to 3 cm in length and 1 to 1.5 cm in diameter. When kept in cold, humid conditions, these seeds can last up to a month. They include a lot of easily absorbed proteins, 40–50% carbs, minerals, vitamins, and phytonutrients including lignans, saponins, and isoflavones that may be good for your health. Every year, 390 kg of seeds can be produced by a single jackfruit tree.

Desired functional properties of the seed flour included bulk density, gelation concentration, and oil absorption capacity. Both native and modified forms of jackfruit starch are extremely promising for novel uses in the food and non-food industries due to their varied structures and functionalities. Jackfruit seed starch is a good alternative to cereal starches in the food industry for uses like soups, creams, and sauces since it has similar properties. Furthermore, the protein found in jackfruit seeds has potential for use in emulsion-based food items. In addition to having desired functional qualities such bulk density, gelation concentration, and oil absorption capacity, jackfruit seeds have strong antioxidant activity.

Numerous culinary products have previously been developed using jackfruit seeds, with encouraging results. The physicochemical characteristics, bioactive components, antioxidant capacity, microstructure, and valorization of jackfruit seed flour in baking and extruded products have all been covered in the few review papers that have been published on the subject thus far. In contrast, it included a thorough rundown of the possible uses of jackfruit seed and jackfruit seed starch in the food and associated industries. integrates research on nutrition, functionality, and industrial applications to provide a modern and thorough viewpoint on the use of jackfruit seeds. The analysis centers on the sustainable use of jackfruit seeds, highlighting how they can assist circular economy activities, cut down on agricultural waste, and improve environmental sustainability.

Jackfruit seeds are well-known for their high protein and carbohydrate content, as well as their abundance in vitamins, minerals, phytonutrients, dietary fiber, numerous bioactive polyphenols, and antioxidants. Magnesium, potassium, phosphorus, sodium, calcium, copper, manganese, iron, and zinc are among the essential minerals they also include. About 10 to 12 percent of the fruit's weight is composed of jackfruit seeds by weight. These seeds are an excellent source of dietary fiber (3.9%) and starch (22%), both of which are healthy for your health. Lignans, isoflavones, saponins, and other phytonutrients with strong anticancer, antioxidant, antiulcer, antihypertensive, and anti-aging properties can be found in the seeds of the jackfruit fruit.

Plants are a rich supply of starch, a complex carbohydrate that is a primary source of energy for humans. For humans, starch is an important source of energy since it is the most widely absorbed form of carbohydrate. In addition to being resistant to temperature, pH, and mechanical shear, starches must be able to hold water and gel. The food industry requires certain qualities. Jackfruit seed is frequently processed to produce a powdered form. A number of processing methods are used to turn the jackfruit seeds into flour or powder. Processing jackfruit seeds improves food's appearance, nutritional content, digestibility, antioxidant qualities, and storage qualities while lowering antinutrient content. Jackfruit seeds are treated in a number of ways, including boiling, drying, and autoclaving.

The practice of altering a food product to raise its value by including new ingredients, using food processing technologies, or improving packaging is known as value addition. Creating more tempting and useful products that consumers find more acceptable and enticing than the original commodities is the main goal. In order to increase their value, value-added foods undergo modifications such as component additions, processing techniques, or novel packaging strategies. Because of its characteristics and nutritional value, jackfruit seeds can be used in a variety of useful ways. With the successive steps of boiling, roasting, or grinding into flour for different recipes, this can be utilized mostly in cooking. Furthermore, jackfruit seeds have a wide range of uses, such as solid-state fermentation. A significant yet underutilized resource, jackfruit seeds can help with a number of sustainability, health, and nutritional issues. These seeds are a useful component for generating nutrient-dense and functional food items since they are high in minerals, dietary fiber, proteins, carbs, and bioactive substances. Potential health advantages of jackfruit seeds include their antioxidant, anti-inflammatory, antidiabetic, and anticancer qualities. (Maanas Sharma *et al.,* 2024).

Additionally, jackfruit peel is used to reduce pollution by cleaning up dyes from contaminated waterways. Utilizing this technology, a green economic model for garbage management can be created. In order to reduce trash and sustainably safeguard the environment, this review examined the viability of using jackfruit waste to create value-added goods. One of the most important, affordable, and renewable materials for the creation of bioproducts is lignocellulose. Valorization is a sustainable and eco-friendly process that turns waste biomass into useful goods or into recovered materials. Several value-added chemical development strategies have been described by researchers in recent years. The pretreatment techniques used to efficiently convert waste biomass into valuable. Numerous elements, such as carbs, proteins, vitamins, minerals, dietary fibre, and phytochemicals, are abundant in jackfruit. Previous research has shown that jackfruit waste is also a great source for a wide range of environmentally friendly industrial goods, including food and feed additives, biofuels, biomaterials, and pharmaceuticals. Physico-chemical, biological, and creative green pretreatment techniques are used to transform jackfruit biomass into products with added value. To make the utilization of jackfruit wastes more focused and functional, it is important to look into more sophisticated genetic and biotechnological approaches. Furthermore, additional research developments are required to alter the current methods by which biorefineries generate a range of value-added products. (Pradeep kumar singh, Neelam Pathak *et al.,* 2022)

Jackfruit seeds nutritional value and antioxidant properties have received attention recently. The phenolic content and antioxidant activity of jackfruit seeds were found to account for more than 70% of the total antioxidant content and activity. Chemicals and natural food additives could be found in jackfruit seeds. Consumption of seeds, which are a good source of nutrients and have therapeutic benefits, should be encouraged to reduce waste and improve nutritional security. In addition to reducing antinutrients in food, processing improves acceptability, nutritional quality, digestibility, antioxidant activity and storage quality (Boris and Bharathi 2020)

The process of increasing the economic value and consumer appeal of an agricultural product by changing or transforming its original state is known as value addition. To increase the value of agricultural produce, various value-adding technologies such as processing and preservation techniques, dehydration and drying technology, freezing technology, packing, labelling, and so on can be applied. The use of the fruit and seed for commercial processing and value addition to convenience foods has a long way to go in terms of marketability and 4 job creation. Despite efforts from a few quarters, jack fruit continues to receive less than the attention it deserves from researchers in terms of the much-needed emphasis on value addition of this versatile crop. As low-cost indigenous and underutilised components of a widely consumed fruit, jackfruit seeds can be processed and used to make nutrient-dense complementary flours. (Satheeshan *et al.,* 2019)

Conclusion:

The jackfruit, originating in South and Southeast Asia, particularly the Western Ghats of India, holds significant global importance as a nutritious and versatile fruit. India stands as the second-largest producer, with Tamil Nadu being a key cultivating region. Despite its widespread presence, commercial jackfruit farming in India is still developing, facing challenges in cultivation, post-harvest management (leading to substantial waste), and marketing. The fruit's biological classification places it in the *Artocarpus* genus, recognized for its sweet flavor and remarkable nutritional profile, including high fiber, vitamins, minerals, and even a notable protein content, making it a valuable meat alternative for vegans and vegetarians. Its adaptability to diverse climates, excluding temperate zones, further underscores its potential.Jackfruit offers significant nutritional value, being rich in dietary fiber, essential vitamins (C and B6), and minerals like potassium and magnesium, driving increasing consumer interest. Its culinary versatility allows its use in both savory and sweet dishes. Furthermore, jackfruit's sustainable cultivation, requiring fewer inputs and adapting to various soil types, makes it an environmentally friendly crop. The rising demand for jackfruit and its products creates economic opportunities for farmers, producers, and exporters, contributing to job creation and revenue generation. Recognizing and addressing the challenges in its value chain, from farming to market, is crucial to fully harness the potential of this significant crop for economic and nutritional benefits.

References:

1. Balamaze, J., Muyonga, J. H., Byaruhanga, Y. B., & Ssekiwoko, F. (2019). Production and utilization of jackfruit (Artocarpus heterophyllus Lam.) in selected districts of Uganda. *Journal of Food Science and Technology*, *56*(3), 1254–1261.
2. Bose, C., & Sabarinath, S. (2024). Jackfruit Seed: A Review on Nutritional Composition, Bioactive Compounds, and Potential Applications. *Journal of Food Biochemistry*, *2024*, 1–12.
3. Chandrakanth Reddy, C., Prabakar, C., Sita Devi, K., Ponnarasi, T., Shelton Peter, Y., & et al. (2019). Constraints in Jackfruit Production, Harvesting and Marketing in Tamil Nadu, India. *International Journal of Current Microbiology and Applied Sciences*, *8*(1), 2640–2647.
4. Chikkanna, G. S., Kumar, A. K. S., Goutam, R., & Kusum, K. (2021). Jackfruit: An Overview on Its Processing and Value Addition. *International Journal of Fruit Science*, *21*(1), 1–16.
5. Islam, S., Begum, R., Khatun, M., & et al. (2015). Jackfruit (Artocarpus heterophyllus L.): A Multipurpose Tree. [1] *Research in Agriculture Livestock and Fisheries*, *2*(2), 233–241
6. Based on the provided text, here are the references in APA 7th edition style that support the information presented in the conclusion:
7. Balamaze, J., Muyonga, J. H., Byaruhanga, Y. B., & Ssekiwoko, F. (2019). Production and utilization of jackfruit (Artocarpus heterophyllus Lam.) in selected districts of Uganda. *Journal of Food Science and Technology*, *56*(3), 1254–1261.
8. Bose, C., & Sabarinath, S. (2024). Jackfruit Seed: A Review on Nutritional Composition, Bioactive Compounds, and Potential Applications. *Journal of Food Biochemistry*, *2024*, 1–12.
9. Chandrakanth Reddy, C., Prabakar, C., Sita Devi, K., Ponnarasi, T., Shelton Peter, Y., & et al. (2019). Constraints in Jackfruit Production, Harvesting and Marketing in Tamil Nadu, India. *International Journal of Current Microbiology and Applied Sciences*, *8*(1), 2640–2647.
10. Chikkanna, G. S., Kumar, A. K. S., Goutam, R., & Kusum, K. (2021). Jackfruit: An Overview on Its Processing and Value Addition. *International Journal of Fruit Science*, *21*(1), 1–16.

CHAPTER 2

SYNTHETIC FOOD DYES AND ITS HEALTH HAZARDS

Lakshmi M and Zareen Fathima

Department of Food Science and Nutrition, Nehru Arts and Science College, Coimbatore, Tamil Nadu-641 105

Introduction:

Food colour considered as an additive and according to the regulation definition, "it is any dye, pigment, or other substance that can impart colour to a food, drug, or cosmetic or to the human body." (FDA,2018). Addition of colorants to foods is thought to have occurred in Egyptian cities, where candy makers around 1500 BC added natural extracts and wine to improve the products appearance. In 1856 the first synthetic colour (mauvine), was developed by Sir William Henry Perkin and the first chemically synthesized colorants were created from aniline in 1900s. Colour is an important characteristic and selection criterion for food choice. Recent studies have highlighted this importance and have shown how selection may change among certain populations, and over time. Colorants are used in the production of soft drinks, candies, chewing gums, chocolates, jelly, bakery products, canned and vegetable products, dairy products, and meat and fish products. There was no control over this use of colour and so inevitably legislation came into force. In particular that was as a result of health concerns over some of the toxic compounds used. An established list of permitted synthetic colours eventually came into force in most countries early in this century. In the last twenty years however, consumers have become increasingly aware of the ingredients in their foods and as such they require foods to be as `natural' as possible. This combined with technological developments has fuelled the increase in the usage of naturally derived colours. Naturally derived colours are usually less stable to heat, light, pH and oxygen. Stability of natural pigments is considered the main challenge to overcome for their utilization as food colorants. They may interact with other ingredients, resulting in the development of unwanted colours and flavours and all hues might not be available. Therefore, this article reviews the scope of some synthetic colours in food processing and increasing the awareness of safety limits of food colorants.(Abdalla S.M. Ammar *et al.,*2021).

When deciding whether to buy or consume a food product, people automatically examine it visually. Color is still one of the most noticeable visual indicators that contributes to the sensory experience of food.According to a large body of research, food color psychologically influences our expectations of flavor before we even taste it. The majority of synthetic food colorants contain dyes from the azo group and are made from chemicals derived from coal tar compounds. Furthermore, synthetic colors like riboflavin that are identical to natural ones are also accessible (Varghese R and Ramamoorthy S, 2023).

Food dyes, synthesized originally from coal tar and now petroleum, have long been controversial because of safety concerns. Many dyes have been banned because of their adverse effects on laboratory animals or inadequate testing. Since prehistoric times, people have been fascinated with colors. From cave paintings to the latest gadgets, color has been a constant companion of humans. Coloring materials aka 'dyes' aren't just for fabrics but have been added to various types of food to enhance their appeal. Evidently, this coloring chemicals have their origin in natural products, which later expanded to the huge market of artificial food dyes. Artificial food colorings have been in the controversy for many years and scrutinized for being possibly linked to cancer, allergies and hyperactivity. Globally, natural as well as artificial dyes are being cautiously researched and regulated by the food safety authorities. In India, the Prevention of Food Adulteration Act, 1954 (now called the Food Safety and Standards Act, 2006), has been implemented for the quality assurance of various types of foods and food products, and only eight dyes have been suggested edible, but within prescribed limits (Jyoti Mittal. 2020).

Prevalence of Prohibited Azo Dyes in Indian Foods

A number of artificial food coloring agents that are prohibited in developed nations are frequently used as food ingredients in India, such as azo dyes, which are toxic and contain one or more azo groups (-N=N-) in their chemical structures. Among the commonly used azo dyes, tartrazine has been shown to have harmful effects on lipid profiles, behavior, liver function, and renal function (Amin and Al-Shehri 2018).

The food industry makes extensive use of food coloring materials to improve the visual appeal of products and increase their consumer appeal. These additives are mainly prized for their capacity to improve the marketability of different foods by adding vivid colors. But in addition to their intended use, food coloring may contain a number of components that are not readily noticeable, which raises questions about how they might affect public health. (Abdalla A Abdalla *et al.,* 2024).

A considerable hike in demand for packaged food fostered the massive use of food colorants. Henceforth, food colorants are added to every packaged and processed food product sold on the markets and almost every food item sold or manufactured by a food industry or a food selling outlet. Additionally, prepared food, e.g. in restaurants and other small food-selling outlets, contains food colouring agents to enhance their visual appeal to entice consumers. However, health hazards reported predominantly in children triggered by these fascinating synthetic colours need to be addressed.In addition, there are also reports on the synergism between colorants and increased incidence of asthma and allergies. Numerous organic dyes are also regarded as micro pollutants in aquatic environments owing to their toxic effects on aquatic life forms and their subsequent consumers in the food chain (Tkaczyk *et al.,* 2020).

Compared to natural colors, synthetic food colors have several economically important properties such as low cost, resistance to light and pH and high color stability. Synthetic food colors are chemicals which originate from coal tar derivatives, and most of them contain an azo-group. Varied foods and beverages available in the market may contain some non-permitted synthetic colors as well as the overuse of permitted synthetic colors. Numerous studies have confirmed that the synthetic food colors are a major source of food intoxication and lead to severe health problems. There are several food additives that had been used extensively in the past but are no longer allowed, due to existing evidence of their side effects, toxicity in the medium and long-term, as well as a high frequency of potential health incidents (Tripathi *et al.,* 2018).

Wider Health Implications of Azo Dyes

The continuously use of permitted synthetic colors is also not safe. The use of non-permitted colors and randomly use of permitted colors are known to provide adverse health effects in the animals and in the humans. The use of food colorants in the production of foods leads to the need for the development of accurate, precise, sensitive, and selective analytical methods for their analysis and quantification (Dey S and Nagababu B, 2019).

Preferred by the industry, synthetic colorants are chemically or physically modified products with desirable characteristics for manufacturing, such as high purity, coloring capacity, stability, brightness, wide range of shades, uniformity and reproducibility in production, and low cost compared to natural colorants. As science has advanced, more artificial colors have been developed that are very stable and allow a wide range of colors, which has led to their increasing use in the food industry. However, despite the continuous research for synthetic compounds, many of them are for humans, and based on the latest discoveries regarding the side effects and toxicity problems of some synthetic dyes, natural alternatives have become more appealing for consumers worldwide. Furthermore, in order to detect the presence of synthetic food colors in food, highly specific methods and procedures have been developed, which also make it possible to determine the probability of side effects and toxicity in the medium- and long-terms Studies have reported that the intake of artificial colorings, mainly nitro derivatives, of the azo type (E102, E110, E122, E123, E124, and E129) can cause some health problems. The European Parliament, in 2008, decreed those foods containing one or more of these color additives must be labeled with the name or the E-number information followed by the warning "may have an adverse effect on activity and attention in children". Tartrazine (E102), a lemon yellow, used in candies, ice cream, cereals, soups, jellies, cakes, soft drinks, and other foods, is one of the most controversial color additives regarding its safety. Obsessive-compulsive disorders and hyperactivity in children have been linked to its intake, as well as its mutagenic capacity, due to its interaction with human serum proteins. In recent studies, administration of tartrazine at ADI levels in mice showed increased lipid oxidation and changes in biochemical markers in brain tissue hematotoxin, immunotoxin effects, renal disorder, and increased DNA abnormalities. Sunset yellow (E110), obtained from petroleum-derived aromatic compounds, has been related to increased pro-inflammatory activity, as have carmoisine (E122), allura red (E129), and ponceau 4R (E124), which also bind to human and bovine serum albumin. Amaranth (E123), a dye that imparts red color to foods such as in candies, ice cream, and beverages, allowed in the EU but banned in the U.S. due to carcinogenicity, has shown a high genotoxic effect on cultured human lymphocyte (Novais C *et al.,* 2022).

Global Variation in Approved Synthetic Food Colors

The number of synthetic colors approved for food use differs from one country to another. For example, FAO / WHO Codex Alimentarius has accepted synthetic food colors 14, European Union (EU) 15, USA 9, Japan 12, Korea 9 and Iran 7. It should be noted that the Joint FAO / WHO Expert Committee on Food Additives (JECFA) is safe only for food additives that have been assigned an Acceptable Daily Intake (ADI). This was determined on the basis of laboratory animal toxicity tests and human clinical studies. ADI is defined as "an estimate of the amount of a food additive expressed by JECFA on a body weight basis that can be ingested daily throughout a lifetime without significant health risk". This factor ranges from 4 mgkg-1 body weight per day for Sunset yellow, Ponceau and Carmoisine to 12.5 mgkg-1 body weight per day for Brilliant Blue for approved colors. However, azo dyes are widely used in foods because of the cytotoxicity of azo dyes and the potential contribution to carcinogenesis/mutagenesis of intestinal microbiota reduction in azo dyes, the use of these dyes is less likely to be recommended . Synthetic colors used in industrialized countries to color foods artificially raise health concerns of various degrees. For example, erythrosine causes cancer in animals and Allura Red, Tartrazine and Sunset Yellow can be carcinogenic. There is also evidence that Brilliant Blue, Allura Red and Tartrazine cause allergic reactions and also genotoxicity of tartazin by rodent and microbiological studies , has been reported. Furthermore, in-vitro studies of Azorbin colors show chromosomal changes in the somatic cells of the rye. Lastly, there is a major concern about the use of these colors with little attention and increased disease in children. (Maryam Zahedi *et al.,*2020).

Synthetically produced dyes in chemical laboratories are called artificial dyes. These are classified under the category of certified coloring agents. Synthetic dyes are divided into two types: (1) primary food colors (tartrazine, quinoline yellow, azorubine, sunset yellow, allura red, erythrosine, brilliant blue, brilliant black) and (2) blended colors (e.g., egg yellow, yolk yellow, orange red, strawberry red, rose pink, raspberry red, coffee brown, chocolate brown, dark chocolate, lime green, apple green, and pea green). These are mainly used in food, pharmaceutical, and cosmetic industries . Primary synthetic colors are the colors that, when mixed together, produce other colors. Blended colors are produced by mixing the primary colors. Artificial dyes are highly dangerous colorants used in the food industry. Over 90% of artificial dyes are manufactured and they are mostly used in foods. Artificial dyes are decorative additives for foods and food-related products, such as ice, candy, cakes, soda, and so forth, for attracting children and adults at parties. Azo dyes, xanthan, chinilin, and antrachinon are artificial dyes. Azo dyes impart strong and intense color to food products. The ingestion of azo dyes leads to intestinal metabolism to generate carcinogenic metabolites. Since the absorption and metabolic profiles of azo dyes are extremely low, the recommended intake of azo dyes is not problematic for individuals. However, recent studies reported the triggering effect on the immune system due to the absorption of azo dyes from tattoos and the interaction of azo dyes with heme protein. Petroleum based artificial coloring agents are cheap and contain neurotoxic chemicals. These are known to cause hyperactivity, skin rashes, migraine, asthma, cancer, behavioral changes, gastric upset, migraines, skin manifestations, sleep disturbances, night terrors, and so forth. The daily consumption of artificial dyes adds toxicity to the human body without any addition of nutritional value. In the 1900s, around 80 artificial dyes were in use. Later on, these coloring agents were disinterested and were removed from the market due to the observation of unidentified health risks in individuals. (Muthusamy Ramesh *et al.,* 2018)

COMMONLY USED FOOD DYE IN FOOD INDUSTRY

A. Tartrazine

Tartrazine (E102) (FD&C Yellow #5, or Yellow 5) is lemon yellow in color and is a type of anionic azo dye. It is soluble in water and the recommended daily intake of tartrazine is 7.5 mg/kg of body weight. It is used to form a yellow color and in combination with brilliant blue it produces green color. The absorption profile of tartrazine is less than 5% and it is predominantly metabolized by gastrointestinal microflora to the easily absorbed metabolites. The substance was found to be an activator of oestrogen receptor. Tartrazine binds with human, as well as bovine serum albumin to form a complex and halts the physiological functions. Further it causes biliary cirrhosis in postmenopausal women. In addition, neurotoxicity and genotoxicity are also observed. However, it has been recommended as safe if the daily intake is limited. Tartrazine is mainly used in food products (flavoured drinks, alcoholic beverages, seasonings, flavoured fermented milk products, desserts, edible ices, flavoured processed cheese, edible cheese rinds, appetizers, fish roe, fish paste, crustacean paste, precooked crustaceans, smoked fish, pastry, fine bakery products, confectionery including breath refreshing and chewing gum, soft drinks, fruit preserves, processed mushy and garden peas (canned), and other foodstuffs).

B. Quinolone yellow

Quinolone yellow is a qunophthalone type of azo dye . The daily intake of quinolone yellow is 10 mg/kg of body weight and the absorption profile is very low (<3%). It has the properties of inhibiting cholinesterase in erythrocytes and plasma pseudocholinesterase. An additional study reported the possible binding toward human serum albumin. The genotoxicity of quinolone yellow was observed in cell line studies at higher concentrations. It has been used in marmalades, jams and jellies, decorations and coatings, pastry and fine bakery products, confectionery including breath refreshing and chewing gum, flavoured fermented milk products, edible cheese rind, flavoured drinks, seasoning, desserts, ice cream, smoked fish, fish roe, fish paste and crustacean paste, shells, cheeses, edible casings, and some alcoholic beverages.

C. Azorubine

The food colouring azorubine is an Azo dye consisting of two naphthalene subunits ($C_{20}H_{12}N_2Na_2O_7S_2$). This synthetic food colour gives a red colour to foodstuffs. This colorant is soluble in water slightly soluble in ethanol solution, but insoluble in vegetable oil. Due to the general stability of Azo dyes, Azorubine is pH and heat stable, and it does not fade away when exposed to light and oxygen.It is mainly used in foods that are heat-treated after fermentation, occurs as red to maroon powder or granules, and is soluble in water and sparingly soluble in ethanol. Azorubine has been used in a large number of foodstuffs, namely flavoured drinks, fruit syrups, canned red fruits, ice creams, flavoured fermented milkproducts, edible ices, desserts, pastry and fine bakery products, confectionery including breath refreshing and chewing gum, soups,sauces, seasoning, seafood, fish roe, fish paste and crustacean paste, precooked crustaceans, appetizers and alcoholic beverages. The recommended daily intake of azorubine is 4 mg/kg of body weight.

D. Sunset yellow

Sunset yellow or orange yellow (E110) is a synthetically coal tar derived azo dye ($C_{16}H_{10}N_2Na_2O_7S_2$). It is mainly used in fermented products, orange squash, orange jelly, marzipan, Swiss roll, apricot jam, citrus marmalade, lemon curd, sweets, and so forth. It also produces a brown color when combined with amaranth. Gastric upset, diarrhea, vomiting, nettle rash (urticaria), and swelling of the skin (angioedema) are the reported adverse effects of sunset yellow. It is banned in Finland and Norway. It has also been linked to hyperactivity in young children.

E. Allura red

Allura red (E129) (FD&C Red Dye #40 or Red 40) is a dark-red, water-soluble, azo dye.Allura red AC, is a synthetic red Azo food colouring with the chemical formula $C_{18}H_{14}N_2Na_2O_8S_2$. It is used as food dye for the replacement of amaranth. Allura red is originally derived from petroleum. It is added into soft drinks, children's medications, and cotton candy. This is the most commonly used dye in the United States for beverages, candies, ice pops, meats, cheeses, salmon, over-the-counter (OTC) medications, and liquid suspensions. Genotoxicity was reported at concentration of 1250 μg/mL at 37°C. The use of this dye has been reduced in food products due to observed health risks, such as decreased concentration, headaches, migraines, hyperactivity, sleep disturbances, and a feeling of skin irritation.

F. Erythrosine

Erythrosine ($C_{20}H_6I_4Na_2O_5H_2O$) is a xanthenedye (thus, it is not an Azo substance) .Erythrosine (E127) is a synthetic food color and is cherry-pink in appearance. It is more widely used in candies, popsicles, and cake-decorating gels. The long-term use has been reported for a cause of thyroid tumor in rat.

G. Brilliant blue

Brilliant blue (E133) is a triarylmethane dye ($C_{16}H_8N_2Na_2O_8S_2$) . it is synthetic and water-soluble dye derived from coal tar.It has a reddish-blue appearance. As a blue dye, it gives green shades when combined with tartrazine. Gastrointestinal absorption of this dye is poor and it is excreted in feces. Brilliant blue is used in the preparation of food items (flavoured drinks, flavoured fermented milk products, edible cheese rinds, seasonings, desserts, edible ices, confectionery),pharmaceuticals (mouthwashes), and cosmetics (soaps and shampoos). It is also used in the identification of water distribution in soil. It causes allergic reactions in asthmatic patients. It is reported that, in high doses, it could cause deposits in the kidneys and lymphatic vessels, and that residues of potentially carcinogenic substances can also occur.

H. Brilliant black

Brilliant black (E151) is a synthetic, water-soluble, diazo dye. It is in the form of sodium ($C_{28}H_{17}N_5Na_4O_{14}S_4$), potassium or calcium salts. It is mainly used for food coatings, desserts, sweets, ice cream, mustard, red fruit jams, soft drinks, flavored milk drinks, fish, paste, and so forth. It acts as a histamine generator and may increase the chance of asthmatic symptoms and allergic reactions.

I. Fast green

Fast green (E143), Green S or Brilliant green BS is a green synthetic coal tar tri-arylmethane food colouring agent in the form of sodium ($C_{27}H_{25}N_2NaO_7S_2$), potassium or calcium salts. The limited quantity (100 mg/kg) is used in tinned green peas, jellies, sauces, fishes, desserts, and dry bakery mixes. It has poor absorption profiles. It has shown mutagenic effect in animals and humans. The adverse effects may include eye irritation, skin irritation, and digestive and respiratory tract irritation.

J. Nitrates and nitrites

Nitrates and nitrites of potassium or sodium are produced from the source of nitrogen,oxygen, and various other organic and inorganic compounds. When these colorants react with saliva or food products produces nitrosamines, which are carcinogenic. These are present in many of the foodstuffs. Nitrates are also used as color fixatives in cured and processed meats, such as bacon, bologna, and frankfurters; and in smoked fish, such as salmon and tuna. (Muthusamy Ramesh *et al.,* 2018)

K. Indigo Carmine

Indigo Carmine (E132) is a blue synthetic dye commonly used in food and pharmaceutical industries. It has been associated with allergic reactions in some individuals. In addition, it has been shown to have toxic effects on cells, including inducing oxidative stress and DNA damage. (Emmanuel Ohifueme Alegbe *et al.,* 2024)

L. Amaranth

The amaranth food colouring is a modified red Azo dye obtained synthetically ($C20H11N2Na3O10S3$) (5). This anionic dye is a reddish-brown powder or granule (soluble in water and sparingly soluble in ethanol) that decomposes at 120 °C without melting. Amaranth is used in the form of a tri-sodium salt, but potassium and calcium salts can also be applied.The use of amaranth is very restricted, being limited to drinks and some alcoholic drinks, including spirits, aperitif wines, and fish roe.An acceptable daily intake of 0.15 mg/kgbw was established for amaranth . Amarnath dye can present health problems, namely allergic reactions, asthma (as it is an histamine liberator), or hives.

M. Ponceau 4R

Ponceau 4R synthetic Azo food colouring that gives a red colour to foodstuffs.This food colour is a reddish powder or granule which is soluble in water and sparingly soluble in ethanol. Ponceau 4R is used as food coloring agent to intensify red colour commonly used in some sausages, flavoured drinks, flavoured fermented milk products, edible ices, desserts, edible cheese rind, fruit syrups, red fruit preserves, jellies, jams and marmalades, pastries and fine baked goods, confectionery including breath refreshing and chewing gum, soups, appetizers, seasonings, sauces, seafood, fish roe, fish paste and crustacean paste, precooked crustaceans, smoked fish, and alcoholic beverages. The acceptable daily intake for ponceau 4R is 0.7 mg/kgbw.

N. Patent blue V

This Azo food colouring Patent blue is a sky-blue synthetic tri-phenyl-methane dye.The use of the potassium salt is also authorized . This food colour usually takes the form of a blue powder or granule, and is soluble in water and slightly soluble in ethanol.It is redox-sensitive, changing from reduced yellow to oxidized red forms in solution.This synthetic colourant has been used in flavoured drinks, decorations and coatings for pastry products, pastry and fine bakery products, confectionery including breath refreshing and chewing gum, flavoured fermented milk products, edible cheese rinds, desserts, edible ices,several types of preserves of red fruits, seasonings, snacks, and alcoholic beverages.

O. Litholrubine bk

Litholrubine BK is an Azo food colouring agent of synthetic origin which is only used to give a red colour to edible cheese rinds. It is a red powder which is slightly soluble in hot water but insoluble in cold water and in ethanol. Some side effects on human health, arising from the consumption of this dye are similar to those of other Azo dyes, (i.e, it is an allergizing substance). Additionally, it is suspected of hyperkinesia, and there is the possibility of having residues of potentially carcinogenic substances. (Ravindra B. Malabadi *et al.,*2022)

P. Rhodamine B

Rhodamine B (RhB) dye is a synthetic dye widely used as a coloring in textiles and food products.It is a bright red organic fluorescent pigment used as a coloring agent in various industries such as textiles, paper, paint, etc. Its high solubility in water and its lowcost nature makes it a commonly used pigment in various industries.It is also used as a dye in production of rose milk.Colors are characterized by complex chemical structures; subsequently, they are non biodegradable. RhB dye, likes other dyes, stable to light, heat, oxidation, and is not biologically degradable.Some studies suggest that RhB dye is considered as carcinogenic and mutagenic origin in animals and humans. It causes biological issues such as skin, respiratory inflammation, hemolysis, degenerative changes in the liver, and kidneys, etc.. (Zainab Mohammad Saigl 2021).

HEALTH HAZARDS OF SYNTHETIC DYE

Artificial food dyes are found in so many foods, they are almost impossible to avoid. Not only are they extremely popular they are also extremely detrimental to people's health. Studies have confirmed that artificial and synthetic food dyes are a major source of food intoxication and cause severe health issues such as attention deficit hyperactivity disorder (ADHD). A study showed that 73% of children who have ADHD showed fewer symptoms of ADHD when artificial food dyes were removed from their diet. It was concluded that food dyes increased the hyperactivity of children in the age range of three to nine. Along with hyperactivity, food dyes, specifically Yellow 5, was shown to cause many other behavioral changes as well including irritability, restlessness, depression, and trouble sleeping.(Sophia Racanelli,2022)

Synthetic food colors have been increasingly used than natural food colors by food manufacturers to attain certain properties such as low cost, improved appearance, high color intensity, more color stability and uniformity. Varied foods and beverages available in the market may contain some non-permitted synthetic colors and over use of permitted synthetic colors. This may lead to severe health problems such as mutations, cancers, reduced hemoglobin concentrations and allergic reactions. Moreover, 60% of the beverages violated the label requirement without including proper color ingredients. Various factors that effect on human health include; the most concerning claim about artificial food dyes is that they cause cancer. However, the evidence to support this claim is weak. Based on the research currently available, it is unlikely that consuming food dyes will cause cancer. Certain food dyes because allergic reactions in some people, but if you do not have any symptoms of an allergy, there is no reason to eliminate them from your diet. The claim about food dyes that has the strongest science to back it up is the connection between food dyes and hyperactivity in children. Several studies have found that food dyes increase hyperactivity in children with and without The reason dyes are used in foods is to make food look more attractive. There is absolutely no nutritional benefit of food dyes. The biggest sources of food dyes are unhealthy processed food that have other negative effects on health. Food dyes are likely not dangerous for most people, but avoiding processed foods that contain dyes can improve your overall health.(Dey S and Nagababu B, 2019).

Food poisoning could result from adulterations. Food illness, fatalities, and even adulterations of synthetic food colors are more likely to occur, especially in youngsters. According to a number of studies, Market- available items like bakery goods, confections, and beverages commonly incorporate artificial food coloring. Market-available foods and beverages may have both an excessive amount of legal artificial colors as well as certain prohibited synthetic colors. Synthetic food colors have been linked to serious health issues like allergies, low hemoglobin levels, genetic abnormalities, irritability, restlessness, effects on the organs, and, hyperactivity in children. Pet food frequently comes in a spectrum of hues, and this is no accident. It's pleasant to see the golden chicken, and the scarlet of rare steak, when you unzip a package since these colors represent the original components' colors, which may lose during the production process. These colors are added after the event. The colors are actually included to attract pet parents because dogs and cats can't see the same range of hues that humans can. The use of these harmful food colors was outlawed by the Food and Drugs Act of 1906. Colors are frequently added to hide rotting or discoloration of food. Even though some food dyes, especially when used in large quantities, might well have cancer-causing effects, are not currently among the colors that the FDA has approved. FDA-approved colors should be harmless in foods for both people and pets if they are used as directed. Animals exposed to semi-toxic concentrations of Sunset blue experience abnormalities in their body's overall lipid storage. This would have an impact on their metabolism and could result in dangerous liver damage including necrosis (Shalini and Saxena, 2023).

The coloring qualities, consistency, stability, and affordability of synthetic dyes make them popular. But many of them turn toxic after long-term use, leading to health issues like indigestion, anemia, and allergic reactions like urticaria and asthma, as well as pathological lesions in the brain, kidney, spleen, and liver, tumors and cancer paralysis, mental retardation, abnormalities in offspring, growth retardation, and eye defects that lead to blindness. In addition to the genotoxic and carcinogenic risks, other health problems include headaches, urticaria, asthma, nausea, eczema, bronchitis, bronchospasm, decreased blood coagulation, and hyperactivity. The majority of natural colorants have certain drawbacks, including instability in water, sensitivity to light and heat, and reactivity to other food ingredients or odors. Furthermore, using natural food coloring can be very beneficial in contrast to using synthetic dyes; their dependability, functionality, biological potential, and health benefits make them popular. In contrast to synthetic dyes, which are created chemically, natural colors are derived from nature and can be separated through somewhat complex extraction procedures. However, it can occasionally be challenging to distinguish between natural and synthetic colors.Our daily diets now include unhealthy processed foods. Over the past 50 years, the amount of artificial food dye consumed has multiplied, with children being the largest consumers. Chemicals that cause cancer may be present in some dyes. Food dyes like tartrazine, erythrosine, and carmoisine are the main contributors to liver cancer. The most popular classes of food dyes that are added illegally are triphenylmethanes and azo dyes. The production of active aromatic amines that attack DNA is the result of enzyme-mediated Azo reduction. As a result, many food products use color to achieve a desirable look or dye feature. For instance, in order to enhance consumers preferences, food colours are usually applied to edible ices, desserts, pastry and fine bakery products, decorations and the coatings of pastry, confectionary products, sauces, fruit juices, snacks and soft drinks, and alcoholic beverages. To enhance the dietary items' visual appeal, a variety of chemical food color and flavor additives are frequently added during processing. However, many of them are toxic after prolonged use.(Ravindra B. Malabadi *et al.,*2022).

Many studies indicate that artificial colors are directly associated with various pathological conditions, such as cancer, food allergies, and gastrointestinal and respiratory problems. Furthermore, behavioral changes in children are described, with the group of children with Autism Spectrum Disorder (ASD) being one of the most impacted by these adversities.The harms of synthetic dyes in children, both with and without comorbidities, are worrying and require a careful and proactive approach. The studies presented in this review demonstrate an association between the consumption of these additives and a variety of adverse health effects, ranging from hyperactivity and behavioral disorders to allergic reactions and more serious health problems. For children with comorbidities such as Autism Spectrum Disorder and Attention Deficit Hyperactivity Disorder, exposure to synthetic dyes can worsen existing symptoms and complicate management of the condition. Furthermore, even in children without comorbidities, synthetic dyes can pose a health risk by affecting their cognitive, behavioral, metabolic and nutritional development. (Zandleme Birino de Oliveira *et al.,*2024).

Natural dyes are biodegradable without the need for any oxidants or reductants, whereas synthetic dyes are very difficult to remove from the industry effluents because they tend to remain fairly stable to common oxidation and reduction processes according to their design. If they degrade at all, synthetic dyes are full of byproducts that have been shown to be harmful to human health either directly or indirectly; these dangerous substances have not yet been found in the byproducts of natural dye degradation. Under natural circumstances, natural dyes might totally deteriorate.Because of their synthetic origin and complex molecular structures, which hinder their ability to biodegrade, synthetic dye-based effluents can pose a serious risk to the environment and water streams. Currently, many synthetic dyes that cause allergies and cancer are limited. Although they have not been outlawed yet, many dyes might not be entirely safe. The majority of synthetic dyes do not biodegrade and end up in rivers and on land, which causes ecological issues. The dyes that contain heavy metals and those that cause cancer have a significant impact and are undesirable. Allergy-causing dyes are not regarded as low impact. Increased heart rate, shock, vomiting, cyanosis, jaundice, quadriplegia, heinz body formation, and tissue necrosis are all possible side effects of cationic dyes. (Sajda.S. Affat, 2021)

Conclusion:

Synthetic food dyes, while enhancing visual appeal and offering economic advantages, pose significant health hazards, particularly in vulnerable populations like children. The use of prohibited azo dyes in some regions, alongside the potential risks associated with even permitted synthetic colors, raises serious concerns. Studies link these additives to hyperactivity, allergies, genotoxicity, and even carcinogenicity. Regulatory bodies differ in their approval lists and ADI levels, highlighting the ongoing debate and the need for stringent monitoring. The increasing consumption of processed foods necessitates greater awareness of these risks and a potential shift towards natural alternatives to safeguard public health. Further research and stricter regulations are crucial to mitigate the adverse effects of synthetic food dyes.

References:

1. Swain, A. R., Dutton, J., & Truswell, A. S. (1985). Salicylates in foods and artificial colors. *The Medical Journal of Australia, 142*(11), 512-513.
2. Carocho, M., Barreiro, M. F., Morales, P., & Ferreira, I. C. F. R. (2014). Adding colour to foods: synthetic versus natural colorants. *Comprehensive Reviews in Food Science and Food Safety, 13*(5), 725-740.
3. Chung, K. T., Stevens, S. E., Jr., & Cerniglia, C. E. (1992). The reduction of azo dyes by human intestinal bacteria. *Critical Reviews in Microbiology, 18*(3), 175-190.
4. Combes, R. D., & Haveland-Smith, R. B. (1982). A review of the genotoxicity of food, drug and cosmetic colours and other azo, triphenylmethane and xanthene dyes. *Mutation Research/Reviews in Genetic Toxicology, 98*(2), 101-248.
5. EFSA Panel on Food Additives and Nutrient Sources added to Food (ANS). (2009). *Scientific Opinion on the re-evaluation of Sunset Yellow FCF (E 110) as a food additive* (EFSA Journal, 7(11), 1331). European Food Safety Authority.

6. EFSA Panel on Food Additives and Nutrient Sources added to Food (ANS). (2010). *Scientific Opinion on the re-evaluation of Tartrazine (E 102) as a food additive* (EFSA Journal, 8(11), 1796). European Food Safety Authority.
7. Kobylewski, S., & Jacobson, M. F. (2012). *CSPI's guide to food additives*. Center for Science in the Public Interest.
8. McCann, D., Barrett, A., Cooper, A., Crumpler, D., Dalen, L., Grimshaw, K., Harley, D., James, J., Stevenson, J., & исследование, Г. Ф. А. С. (2007). Food additives and hyperactive behaviour in 3-year-old and 8/9-year-old children in the community: a randomised, double-blind, placebo-controlled trial. *The Lancet*, *370*(9598), 1560-1567.
9. Shimada, H., Tanaka, A., Kojima, M., Kamata, E., & Imamura, S. (2010). Effects of food coloring Tartrazine on allergic inflammation in NC/Nga mice. *Journal of Immunotoxicology*, *7*(1), 81-87.
10. Stevens, L. J., Kucera, E., Burgess, J. R., Stochelski, M. A., Arnold, L. E., & Galland, L. (2011). Mechanisms of behavioral, neuroendocrine, and immunologic effects of food additives in children with attention-deficit/hyperactivity disorder. *Behavioral and Brain Functions*, *7*(1), 31.

CHAPTER 3

FUNCTIONAL APPLICATION OF LIGNIN FROM CHRYSOPOGON ZIZANIOIDES

Jyothika Das P

Department of Food Science and Nutrition, Nehru Arts and Science College, Coimbatore, Tamil Nadu-641 105

Introduction

Vetiver is a traditional plant that has many uses in agriculture, medicine, fragrance, commerce, and environmental protection. Chrysopogon zizanioides is a member of the species-diversified Poaceae family, which has 11,337 species and 707 genera. The perennial, evergreen grass Chrysopogon zizanioides grows in clumps that are 1 to 1.5 meters tall, and occasionally as tall as 3 meters. Its roots can reach a depth of 3–4 meters in the first year of cultivation and grow very quickly under ideal conditions, which helps them survive harsher climates like drought and floods.Various parts of vetiver have been used for centuries for their numerous medicinal benefits, in addition to their use as a species for wastewater treatment and soil conservation. Vetiver is classified as Mutrala (which improves urinary excretion), Shukra Shodhana (which treats genital disorders like urinary calculi, dysuria, spermatorrhea, etc.), and Dahaprashamana (which lessens fatigue) in the ancient ayurvedic text Charaka Samhita. In contrast to other parts, vetiver roots are highly valued in Ayurveda, which uses their properties as a blood purifier to remove excess toxins from the body, which acts as a cardioprotective; a gastrointestinal system strengthener by reducing indigestion and excessive acid production; and a remedy for digestive issues (such as diarrhea and anorexia); and respiratory issues (such as cough, asthma, and tuberculosis). In addition, it is used as a sedative, energizer, nervine tonic, antidepressant, and sexual desire stimulant.It is also good for anemia because it improves blood circulation.For rheumatoid arthritis, lumbago, and sprains, the plant's root and leaf mixture also relieves pain. The distilled root oil can also be used as a refresher in an oil diffuser. (Madhuri Grover *et al.,* 2021)

In Traditional Medicine, Different portions of the vetiver plant are used by different people to treat a wide variety of conditions, including mouth ulcers, boils, epilepsy, burns, snake bites, scorpion stings, rheumatism, fever, headaches, and more. A decoction of the roots has been used as a tonic for weakness, while the Santhal people of Bihar and West Bengal, India, utilize the paste made from fresh roots to treat burns, snakebites, and scorpion stings. The Lodhas of the West Bengal region utilizes a paste made from the plant's roots to treat conditions like headaches, rheumatism, and sprains. A decoction made from the plant's stems is taken to treat UTIs. Leaf juice is used as an anthelmintic by the tribal people of Madhya Pradesh's Mandla and Bastar regions. It is also effective against mouth sores, snakebites,scorpion stings, fever, and epilepsy.

Pain in the head and teeth can be relieved by a root extract. Tribal people in Varanasi, India, treat malaria by inhaling the vapor from the root. The Oraon people use root ash to treat acidity. In the same way, the plant has a wide variety of medical uses among India's diverse ethnic. (Madhuri grover *et al.,*2020)

FUNCTIONAL PROPERTIES OF CRYSOPOGON ZIZANIOIDES

a. Anti-Oxidant Activity

Lipid peroxidation and DNA damage are caused by free radicals. It has been demonstrated that certain plant extracts possess antioxidant properties that can counteract free radicals in living things. Chrysopogon zizanioidesis has the highest antioxidant content. Chrysopogon zizanioidesis a tufted grass that is commonly used in aromatherapy to treat stress, anxiety, nervous tension, and sleeplessness.

b. AntitubercularActivity

The antimicrobial activity of vetiver grass (Chrysopogon zizanioides) root extracts against Mycobacterium tuberculosis was quite strong. In particular: 500 µg/mL ethanolic extracts demonstrated notable antituberculosis properties.Hexane fractions (50 µg/mL) inhibited Mycobacterium tuberculosis growth.

c. Hepatoprotective Activity

Hepatoprotective effects have been shown for Chrysopogon zizanioides extracts in both methanol and ethanol. At dosages of 300–500 mg/kg, an extract made from this grass and prepared with methanol has demonstrated effectiveness. 20% toxicity was caused by ethanol extract at 3.7 mg/kg.

d. Antibacterial Activity

Chrysopogon zizanioides contains antibacterial flavonoids, alkaloids, terpenoids, saponins, tannins, and phenols.inhibited gram-negative bacteria more than grampositive bacteria. The ability of phytochemicals to combine with soluble and extracellular proteins as well as the bacterial cell wall makes them excellent antimicrobials that are compatible with a wide range of microorganisms.Microbial membranes may be ruptured by more lipophilic flavonoids. Tannins are antibacterial because they bind with polysaccharides and eliminate the transport proteins in the cell membrane as well as the enzymes that bacteria use to adhere to one another.

e. Antihyperglycaemic Activity

An ethanolic root extract of Vetiveria zizanioides has been shown to have antihyperglycemic properties. This extract was beneficial to rats in standard laboratory settings. (Indrajeet Singh *et al.,* 2023)

f. Anti-fungal Activity

Antifungal drugs are commonly used to treat infections caused by fungi. Fungal infections on the skin usually do not pose a threat to life, but when they spread inside the body and endanger vital organs, they can be dangerous. Vetiveria zizanioides extracts, both aqueous and ethanolic, killed the normal cultures of Aspergillus nigra, Aspergillus clavatus, and Candida albicans.The griseofulvin and nystatin agar plate method was used for standardization.(Oliveira TAS *et al.,* 2022).

f. Antiseptic activity

The hot, humid climate found in tropical areas is ideal for the growth of bacteria and other microorganisms. This oil effectively prevents the growth of the bacteria that causes septicemia, Septicemia aureus, and eliminates them, which helps treat septicemia and protects against it. (Ankit Pandey & S C Tiwari, 2023).

g. Antileishmanial activity

According to these results, the plant's bioactive compound may be used as a component of innovative dental care products and may also be browbeaten for use in leishmaniasis research and the development of new drugs. Leishmaniaama zonensis can be effectively controlled by the aromatic component that is extracted from C. zizanioides roots (Fampa P *et al.,* 2022).

STRUCTURE AND FUNCTIONAL PROPERTIES OF LIGNIN

Lignin is another polymer of interest for biobased, in addition to cellulose. It is the second most prevalent polymer (15–30%) in lignocellulosic biomass and yields multipurpose compounds with high potential for value addition as byproducts of pulping or the production of bioethanol from lignocellulose. The heterogeneous polymer lignin is found in plant cell walls and is crosslinked with cellulose and hemicellulose. This resistant polymer has thus been extracted from the cell wall and transformed into aromatic products of industrial interest by a number of chemical and enzymatic methods utilizing sophisticated oxidative reactions. Consequently, depending on the kind and intensity of the removal process, the chemical properties of the isolated raw material are different from those of native lignin. A few of these features include the distribution of molar mass, the amount of monomer units, the pattern of intermonomer linkages (S, G, H), the quantity of functional groups (like phenol, alcohol, or methoxy groups), and the presence of new groups like sulfonate groups that are created during the process. Additionally, the phenolic fraction is somewhat tainted by carbohydrates, which either dissolve with lignin or remain as a byproduct of the conversion of lignocellulose.(E. Gerbin, 2021)

The sustainable production of renewable fuels, chemicals, and materials for human use is made possible by the abundant supply of lignocellulosic biomass. For thousands of years, wood, in particular, has been utilized as a fuel source for heating and as a building and construction material for a variety of purposes. The cell walls of plants contain the majority of their mass and are mainly made up of the alkylaromatic heteropolymer lignin and the polysaccharides cellulose, hemicellulose, and pectin. The three fundamental components of lignin—p-coumaryl alcohol, coniferyl alcohol, and sinapyl alcohol—are produced in plants through the phenylpropanoid pathway and vary in the degree of methoxylation they contain (0, 1, and 2, respectively). These monomers are enzymatically dehydrogenated to create lignin, which has a three-dimensional, heterogeneous structure and forms both C–O and C–C bonds. Additional lignin constituents like flavonoids and hydroxycinnamic acids, which are briefly covered below, add more linkages and chemical functionality to the aromatic heteropolymer while also further complicating its structure. (RUI KATAHIRA *et al.,* 2018).

Lignin is thought to have the capacity to stabilize reactions initiated by oxygen free radicals by acting as a scavenger of these radicals. There are many different aromatic compounds found in lignin. It is made up of three different phenylpropane monomers and contains a high concentration of phenolic hydroxyl groups and benzene rings.These aromatic moieties give lignin its UV-absorbing properties, making it not only oxidation-resistant but also an ultraviolet protective agent. Other research groups have already investigated the antioxidant qualities of lignin. assessed the antioxidant properties of several organosolv lignin samples made under varied circumstances using the response surface method. The results showed that lignin with a lower molecular weight and more phenolic hydroxyl groups had higher antioxidant activity. The extracted lignin demonstrated strong antioxidant activity based on the hydrophilic oxygen radical absorbance capacity assay and the modified Folin–Ciocalteu test.(Jia Xu *et al.,*2020).

The complex organic polymer class known as lignin is found in the structural tissues of plants. The properties of lignin can differ depending on its origin, such as polydispersity molar masses and hyperbranched structures. Lignin is created by the oxidative coupling of monolignols, which are generated by the phenyl propanoicells pathway. In plants, especially in larger roots and stems, lignin mainly provides rigidity by strengthening the cell wall structure. It provides a Young's modulus of 2.5–3.7 GPa and an additional 25–74 MPa of tensile strength. Lignin regulates the flow of liquids through the plant, including water. In addition, it offers defense against biological stressors by stopping the enzymatic degradation of other substance. Lignin contains antioxidants, which are discussed in greater detail later in the book, and provides the plant with defense against microbes. Lignin also gives the cell walls of some plant cell types their waterproof quality. Certain cell walls will lignify as part of their regular processes as they become more specialized. However, certain cell walls that would not typically lignify can do so as a result of internal biotic and abiotic stressors. Different kinds of lignin are produced by plants, depending on the species and the connections formed between phenylpropane units. The structure of the three-dimensional network in lignin is random. Furthermore, the percentage of lignin varies from 15 to 40 percent depending on the species. The amount of lignin in the same species also varies by a few percentage points. There is also variation in the amount of lignin in plants; wood has been found to have a higher lignin content, while young shoots have a very low lignin content. A study of the lignin content of Eucalyptus globulus plants found that

P-hydroxyphenyl (H), guaiacyl (G), and syringyl (S) are deposited later in growth and that the lignin composition of the plant changes with age. The phenolic compounds H, G, and S are found in lignin and its structure; they affect the interunit bonds that lignin molecules form with one another. Another study found a negative correlation between increased biomass as the tree grows and the regulation and production of lignin in larger trees. This is due to the competition for carbon between cellulose, hemicellulose, and lignin.Lignin can be classified according to its resources. Gymnosperm (softwood) lignin is made up of more than 90% guaiacyl units for the seeded vascular phyla, while angiosperm (hardwood) lignin is a copolymer of guaiacyl and syringyl units of varying ratios. Vascular, seedless plants (grass) are even more like angiosperms due to their different ratios of guaiacyl and syringyl units. There are three different kinds of lignin that can be extracted from wood: milled wood lignin (MWL), dioxane lignin, and cellulolytic enzyme lignin (CEL). Kraft lignin, soda lignin, and lignosulfonates are byproducts of chemical pulping that are created by additional processing in the paper industry. As mentioned above, the seeds, leaf type, and reproductive strategy of the plant are what differentiate gymnosperms from angiosperms. They do not always have higher lignin contents than each other.

APPLICATION OF LIGNIN TO REDUCE TOXICITY OF FOOD DYE

Low availability of non-renewable resources is the most concerning issue worldwide. Petrochemical resources are being used at a high pace due to over-dependency on fossil fuels. So, there is a need to find an alternative for it that is more likely to be renewable, eco-friendly, cost-effective, biodegradable, and sustainable. Lignocellulosic biomass is the best fit to serve this purpose and can be used as a starting material for various bio adsorbents. The second most abundant natural polymer is lignin, comprising up to 10-25 % of lignocellulosic biomass. It is water-insoluble, potentially stable, and acts as the connecting link between cellulose and hemicellulose . Most experiments are performed with lignin as a biopolymer because of its plentiful availability on earth. At present, lignin is under-used, and its potential is not well articulated. In addition to its natural occurrence, lignin can be produced by chemical activities such as sulfonation, oxidation, graft copolymerization, hydroxymethylation reactions. lignin can be used for various purposes, such as removing dyes toxicity and heavy metals. lignin-based composites had shown high activity for the processes in the field of photocatalytic remediation, such as oxidation and desulphurization of organic dyes. Lignin-based nanoparticles are considered the most efficient adsorbents due to their physicochemical characteristics. The higher surface area, efficiency, and low-cost production make it an effective alternative for removing dye. (Anubhuti Bhatia *et al.*,2021)

The increasing use of synthetic food colorants has raised concerns due to their potential health risks, including allergic reactions, hyperactivity, and carcinogenic effects. Synthetic dyes such as Allura Red AC, Tartrazine, and Rhodamine B are widely used in processed foods to enhance their visual appeal but have been linked to toxicological concerns (Oplatowska-Stachowiak & Elliott, 2019).

The availability of plentiful hydroxyl groups in lignin macromolecules and its unique three-dimensional structure make it an ideal precursor for mesoporous biosorbents.complex polymer of aromatic alcohols containing abundant functional groups, lignin shows potential capacities for the sorption of heavy-metal-ions. Up to now, various lignin-based biosorbents have been fabricated and successfully used to remove heavy-metal-ions from aqueous solution. The unique structure of the lignin may provide large surface area and large pore volume, and possess better diffusion, dispersion, and mass transfer behavior in the field of heavy-metal-ions removal (Fang Xu *et al.,* 2016). It have excellent biodegradability and outstanding low toxicity. Meanwhile, it is also an amorphous aromatic polymer with a certain number of active groups, such as hydroxyl (-OH) and carboxyl (-COOH) groups. Therefore, it is regarded as an ideal material for the production of renewable adsorbent to solve the problem of heavy metal ion pollution. (Nadia Fattahi *et al.,*2024)

Lignin has been explored as a potential adsorbent to reduce the toxicity of food dyes. lignin-based adsorbents have shown promising results in removing food dyes, such as methylene blue and rhodamine B, from aqueous solutions. The lignin's high surface area, functional groups, and porous structure, which enable it to effectively adsorb and remove the dye molecules. Furthermore, the article highlights the potential of lignin-based adsorbents to be used as a sustainable and eco-friendly solution for reducing the toxicity of food dyes in food products and wastewater (Kumar *et al.,* 2020). Lignin, a complex organic polymer, has gained significant attention for its adsorption properties, particularly in wastewater treatment and heavy metal removal. Recent studies have explored the modification methods of lignin adsorbents, including surface modification with nitrogen, oxygen, and sulfur functional groups, as well as composite modification. The adsorption mechanisms of lignin involve electrostatic attraction, and hydrogen-bond interaction, making it an effective material for removing toxic pollutants. Lignin-based adsorbents have shown promise in removing heavy metals, such as mercury and lead, from wastewater, with some studies reporting adsorption capacities comparable to commercial adsorbents. Overall, lignin's adsorption properties make it a valuable material for environmental remediation and wastewater treatment applications. (Tong Wang *et al.,* 2022)

Lignin-based hydrogels have shown potential in detoxifying food dyes, such as methylene blue, through adsorption. The hydrogel's porous structure and functional groups, such as hydroxyl and phenolic groups, enable it to interact with and remove the dye molecules. This application highlights the potential of lignin-based hydrogels in promoting sustainable agriculture and reducing environmental pollution.(Antonio Di Martino *et al.,* 2022)

Conclusion

Vetiver is a remarkably versatile plant with a rich history of traditional uses spanning medicine, agriculture, and beyond. Its various parts have long been valued for their therapeutic properties. Modern scientific inquiry has begun to validate these traditional uses, revealing a range of beneficial activities.Furthermore, the exploration of plant-derived materials like lignin offers a promising and sustainable approach to tackling contemporary environmental and health concerns. Lignin's unique properties make it a potential solution for mitigating the toxicity of synthetic food dyes, highlighting the value of investigating natural resources for addressing modern challenges.

Reference

1. Carocho, M., Barreiro, M. F., Morales, P., & Ferreira, I. C. F. R. (2015). Adding value to *Vetiveria zizanioides* L. Nash: A comprehensive review on its multiple applications. *Industrial Crops and Products*, *76*, 894-916.
2. Das, S., Haldar, S., & Pramanik, P. (2018). A review on the pharmacological and cosmeceutical applications of *Vetiveria zizanioides* essential oil. *Journal of Essential Oil Research*, *30*(5), 305-316.
3. Ferreira, A. S., Santos, S. A. O., & Rodrigues, A. E. (2021). Lignin valorization towards bio-based chemicals: A review on depolymerization methods. *Chemical Engineering Journal*, *417*, 127948.
4. Gerbin, E., Kremer, S., & Meier, M. A. R. (2021). From plant to polymer: Sustainable materials based on lignin. *Progress in Polymer Science*, *114*, 101355.
5. Hasan, M. S., Sardar, M. R. I., Shafin, A. A., Rahman, M. S., Mahmud, M., & Hossen, M. M. (2023). A brief review on applications of lignin. *Journal of Chemical Reviews*, *5*(1), 1-11.
6. Kumar, R., Butreddy, A., Kommineni, N., Reddy, P. G., Bunekar, N., Sarkar, C., Dutt, S., Mishra, V. K., & Aadil, K. R. (2021). Lignin: Drug/gene delivery and tissue engineering applications. *PMC*. Retrieved from [Insert relevant PMC link if available]
7. Lievonen, M., Toikka, M., & Karvonen, L. (2023). Functional surfaces, films, and coatings with lignin – a critical review. *RSC Advances*, *13*(36), 24683-24701.
8. Swain, A. R., Dutton, J., & Truswell, A. S. (1985). Salicylates in foods and artificial colors. *The Medical Journal of Australia*, *142*(11), 512-513.
9. Wang, T., Zhang, Y., & Chen, Y. (2022). Lignin-based adsorbents for heavy metal removal from wastewater: A review. *Bioresource Technology*, *344*, 126173.
10. Xu, J., Zhou, Y., & Man, Y. (2020). Antioxidant properties of lignin: A brief review. *BioResources*, *15*(1), 1924-1939.

CHAPTER 4

STRUCTURAL AND FUNCTIONAL PROPERTIES OF CHITIN

Diya Sajid

Department of Food Science and Nutrition, Nehru Arts and Science College, Coimbatore, Tamil Nadu-641 105

Introduction

Chitin is the second most abundant biopolymer on Earth after cellulose, produced by various organisms, including crustaceans, mollusks, insects, and some fungi (Shamshina JL *et al.,* 2019). Despite its massive natural production—estimated at 8–10 billion tons annually—most chitin remains underutilized due to its classification as waste material (Yadav M *et al.,* 2019).

As a fundamental structural biopolymer in the animal kingdom, chitin has an extensive evolutionary history, dating back to the first chitin-producing ancient fungi that emerged on Earth (Loron *et al.,* 2019). However, its potential for technical and industrial applications remains largely untapped. The ancient origin of chitin has been demonstrated in fossilized filaments of eukaryotic organisms found in dolomitic shale dating back 810 to 715 million years (Bonneville *et al.,* 2020). This highlights chitin's long-standing role as a structural biopolymer in nature. Chitin is a valuable resource due to its lightweight and strong properties. Following nature's design principles, we can explore its diverse functionalities through material constructs at different scales. Unlike isolated pure polymers, chitin naturally exists as a nanocomposite material in various crystalline conformations. These structural variations contribute to a range of remarkable optical and mechanical effects in different organisms. For example, chitin-based structures form antireflective arrays in cicada wings (Wang Z *et al.,* 2020), enhance the exceptional mechanical strength of mantis shrimp exoskeletons, and create partially organized fibrils with flexible properties in mushrooms. This versatility makes chitin an important biomaterial for various applications. Organisms utilize chitin's basic fiber units as structural building blocks, tailoring their assembly to specific biological functions. Through biosynthesis, chitin fibrils organize into different conformations, such as long, thin microfibrils or rod-like entities. These variations in structural arrangement suggest that specific forms of chitin contribute to the wide range of mechanical and functional properties observed in nature (Hou J *et al.,* 2021).

The shellfish processing industry generates vast amounts of shell waste, which, if not properly managed, can lead to serious environmental hazards. Globally, an estimated 3.4 million tons of shrimp are harvested annually, with many Asian countries heavily involved in shrimp production (Tolesa LD *et al.,* 2019). Waste generation varies by species, with deep-sea shrimp producing significantly more waste (62.6–65.6%) compared to shallow-water shrimp (40–50%). Shrimp shell waste typically contains 20–30% chitin, 30–50% minerals, and 30–40% proteins, along with small amounts of pigments and lipids (Liu Y *et al.,* 2020). The yield of chitin from different marine crustacean shells depends on the species, generally ranging between 17.50% and 23.75%. Chitin color can vary from white to pink, depending on the source. Abdou et al. isolated chitin from six shell sources, including pink and brown shrimp, squid pens, freshwater lobsters, and crabs, using 1 M HCl and 1 M NaOH treatments. They found that chitin from squid pens was white, while chitin from other sources exhibited a pink hue (Rasweefali, M.K *et al.,* 2022).

Challenges of Interference from Associated Biomolecules

Chitin detection has historically been problematic due to its natural occurrence as a compound tightly bound to other substances such as polysaccharides, lipids, proteins, pigments, and biominerals like calcium carbonate ($CaCO_3$) or silica, which are found in various skeletal structures (Tsurkan MV *et al.,* 2020). The primary method for identifying chitin has involved chemically or enzymatically removing these interfering substances to obtain purified chitin (Klinger *et al.,* 2019; Pighinelli, 2019). Chitin, with the molecular formula $(C_8H_{13}O_5N)_n$, is a linear polymer composed of N-acetyl-D-glucosamine (N-acetyl-2-amino-2-deoxy-D-glucose) units linked by β-1,4-glycosidic bonds. It also contains a small proportion of deacetylated monomer units (2-amino-2-deoxy-D-glucose), which can influence its structural and functional properties. The first chemical structure of chitin was proposed by Meyer and Mark in 1928 (Tsurkan MV *et al.,* 2020). On the evolutionary scale, chitin is considered to be positioned between cellulose and collagen. As a native biopolymer, chitin is semi-crystalline and occurs in fibrous crystalline states, forming different polymorphic structures. The semi-crystalline nature of chitin arises from its hierarchical organization, where polymer chains assemble into alternating amorphous and crystalline regions. These structures are stabilized by hydrogen bonds and van der Waals forces, contributing to chitin's rigidity and functionality (Ling S *et al.,* 2018).

Further structural analysis has identified three distinct polymorphic forms of chitin—α-chitin, β-chitin, and γ-chitin—each differing in the arrangement of their polymeric chains (Tsurkan MV *et al.,* 2020). α-Chitin has an antiparallel chain arrangement, making it the most stable and abundant form. This structure enhances the polymer's rigidity and stiffness, commonly found in crustacean shells, insect exoskeletons, and fungal cell walls. β-Chitin features a parallel chain arrangement, leading to weaker intermolecular interactions but stronger intramolecular hydrogen bonds. This results in a more flexible and less rigid structure, typically found in squid pens, diatom spines, and pogonophoran tubes. γ-Chitin consists of a combination of parallel and antiparallel chains, integrating properties from both α- and β-chitin. It is commonly found in fungi, yeasts, and insect cocoons (T. Hahn *et al.,* 2020). These polymorphic structures contribute to chitin's unique physical and chemical properties. However, upon deacetylation to chitosan, chitin typically loses its crystallinity and becomes amorphous. Chitosan can regain a crystalline phase through hydrolysis in HCl (Tsurkan MV *et al.,* 2020). Pure chitin exhibits strong resistance to alkaline treatment, maintaining its structure even under harsh chemical conditions such as 1M NaOH, whereas other biopolymers degrade. This property has made gravimetric analysis the traditional method for quantifying chitin, where the biopolymer is isolated and weighed after alkaline treatment (Bradić *et al.,* 2020). However, exposure to strong alkaline conditions (>1M NaOH with heating) or highly acidic conditions (>3M HCl with heating) leads to deacetylation and partial fragmentation, converting chitin into chitosan. Since the 1950s, advancements in structural, spectroscopic, and chromatographic methods have improved chitin analysis. These methods have been widely explored for both industrial applications (Lopes *et al.,* 2018) and food research, particularly for quality assurance and contamination detection (Tsurkan MV *et al.,* 2020).

Chemical extraction

Crab and shrimp shells are among the most common commercial sources of chitin, where it remains bound to proteins and minerals in the exoskeleton. The primary mineral in shrimp shells is calcium carbonate ($CaCO_3$), with magnesium being the second most abundant (Knidri HE *et al.,* 2018). Chitin extraction from shell waste can be carried out using three main methods: Chemical methods – involve acid and alkaline treatments to remove minerals (demineralization) and proteins (deproteinization), Enzymatic methods – utilize proteolytic and demineralizing enzymes to achieve the same purpose with milder conditions, Microbiological methods – rely on bacteria that produce organic acids and proteases, offering an eco-friendly alternative (Liu Y *et al.,* 2020).

Chemical extraction is a widely used method for chitin recovery because it provides rapid extraction and ensures almost complete removal of organic salts and proteins from shell waste. The process involves three key steps: Deproteinization – Proteins are removed using strong bases such as sodium hydroxide (NaOH) or potassium hydroxide (KOH), often at elevated temperatures, Demineralization – Minerals, primarily calcium carbonate ($CaCO_3$), are dissolved using acids such as hydrochloric acid (HCl), acetic acid (CH_3COOH), nitric acid (HNO_3), or sulfuric acid (H_2SO_4), Decolorization/Bleaching – Pigments and other impurities are removed to obtain pure chitin (Oyatogun GM *et al.,* 2020). This method is highly efficient but can produce chemical waste, prompting interest in greener enzymatic and microbial alternatives.

Chitin's low solubility in most organic solvents is due to its strong intra- and intermolecular hydrogen bonding, which stabilizes the polymer chains and makes dissolution challenging. However, a few solvents have been identified that can effectively break these interactions. Some organic solvents, such as DMAc-LiCl (Dimethylacetamide-Lithium Chloride) and hexafluoroacetone, have been reported to dissolve chitin, but their practical applications are often limited due to their toxicity and processing challenges. In recent years, ionic liquids (ILs) have emerged as promising solvents for chitin dissolution, as they can disrupt hydrogen bonds and dissolve macromolecules efficiently. Several ILs, including 1-allyl-3-methylimidazolium chloride ([AMIMCl]), 1-allyl-3-methylimidazolium bromide ([AMIMBr]), 1-butyl-3-methylimidazolium chloride ([BMIMCl]), and 1-ethyl-3-methylimidazolium chloride ([EMIMCl]), have demonstrated significant potential in dissolving chitin. Among them, 1-butyl-3-methylimidazolium acetate ([BMIMAc]) and 1-butyl-3-methylimidazolium chloride ([BMIMCl]) are the most widely used due to their effective acetate and chloride anions, which efficiently break chitin's hydrogen bonds. The tunability of ILs, achieved through the independent selection of cations and anions, allows for optimizing their dissolution capacity for chitin and other macromolecules, making them a valuable tool for chitin processing and modification. Chitin is a polymer with low reactivity and is nearly insoluble in most solvents, except for the expensive and toxic combination of dimethylacetamide (DMAc) with lithium chloride (LiCl) (Kritchenkov *et al.*, 2021). Its poor solubility presents significant challenges in various applications. Currently, there are two main categories of solvents used for dissolving chitin: aqueous and non-aqueous. Among non-aqueous solvents, LiCl/DMAc and saturated calcium chloride dihydrate ($CaCl_2 \cdot 2H_2O$) in methanol have been commonly utilized (Wang *et al.*, 2021).

Solvent Systems for Chitin Dissolution

These solvents work by disrupting the hydrogen bonding network within chitin, facilitating its dissolution. However, due to economic and environmental concerns, researchers continue to explore more sustainable alternatives, such as ionic liquids, which show promising potential in enhancing chitin's solubility. Aqueous solvents for chitin dissolution can be categorized into three main types: strong acid solutions, inorganic salt solutions, and alkaline solutions. (1) Chitin dissolves in highly concentrated hydrochloric, sulfuric, and phosphoric acid solutions; however, this process significantly reduces its molecular weight and increases the degree of deacetylation, leading to poor material properties. Additionally, the extensive use of acids raises environmental concerns due to pollution. (2) Chitin has also been observed to dissolve in inorganic salt solutions such as lithium thiocyanate (LiSCN), calcium chloride ($CaCl_2$), and sodium iodide (NaI). However, research on these solvents remains limited, and their dissolution mechanisms are not yet well understood. (3) Among these options, alkaline solvent systems have gained attention due to their milder dissolution conditions and high solubility. Chitin exhibits good solubility in alkali metal/urea systems, including potassium hydroxide (KOH), sodium hydroxide (NaOH), and lithium hydroxide (LiOH) combined with urea. The freezing and thawing process facilitates interactions between chitin and alkali metals through electrostatic forces and hydrogen bonding, weakening intermolecular attractions. At the same time, urea molecules prevent chitin aggregation, allowing for effective dissolution. This synergistic effect between urea and alkali metals enhances chitin solubility in aqueous alkaline solutions (Wang *et al.,* 2021).

Several factors influence the solubility of chitin, including its degree of acetylation (DA), the pH of the solution, temperature, ionic strength, and crystal structure, whereas molecular weight (Mw) does not significantly impact solubility (El Knidri *et al.,* 2020). Interestingly, regenerated chitin with 50% deacetylation, derived from an alkali chitin solution, exhibits excellent solubility in water. This enhanced solubility can be attributed to partial deacetylation and a reduction in molecular weight under alkaline conditions. The distribution of acetyl groups plays a crucial role in determining water solubility when the acetylation degree reaches 50%. However, chitin's inherent insolubility in water, most organic solvents, and dilute acids or alkalis is primarily due to its extensive intra- and intermolecular hydrogen bonding network, which strengthens its structural integrity (Knidri *et al.,* 2018).

Emerging Sustainable Alternatives: The Potential of Ionic Liquids

The crystallinity, crystal structure, and glucosamine content of partially deacetylated chitin are closely linked to its solubility. For instance, chitin with a degree of deacetylation (DD) of 28% is soluble in dilute acetic acid, whereas at a DD of 49%, it becomes soluble in water, indicating that homogeneous deacetylation alters the crystal structure of chitin. Similarly, treatment with strong aqueous hydrochloric acid enhances chitin's solubility by inducing a solid-state transformation of β-chitin into α-chitin. Additionally, the molecular weight (Mw) of chitin is a critical factor influencing its applications across various industries (Rasweefali *et al.,* 2022).

Properties such as viscosity, emulsification, elasticity, adsorption on solids, tear strength, and biofunctional activities are all affected by chitin's molecular weight, making it an essential parameter in determining its functional uses (Pakizeh *et al.,* 2021). Chitin is insoluble in water due to its strong intermolecular hydrogen bonding. However, certain chitin-based derivatives, such as chitosan and carboxymethyl chitin, are water-soluble and offer significant advantages in terms of flexibility. These derivatives can be molded into various forms, including fibers, hydrogels, beads, sponges, and membranes, making them highly versatile. Chitin's crystalline nature contributes to its exceptional tensile strength, which surpasses that of many manufactured materials. This strength is primarily attributed to the extensive hydrogen bonding within chitin's molecular chains. Furthermore, a substantial presence of chitin is found in nearly all fungi, indicating its widespread distribution across the fungal kingdom as well as in the phylum Arthropoda and Mollusca within the animal kingdom (Rameshthangam *et al.,* 2018).

The degree of acetylation (DA) refers to the number of acetyl groups present in the chitin polymer. In native chitin, most C-2 amino groups are acetylated, while some remain free. DA plays a crucial role in determining not only the solubility

of chitin but also its physical, chemical, and biological properties. The extent of N-acetylated amino groups varies depending on the species from which chitin is derived and the methods used for its extraction. Additionally, the extraction process itself can significantly impact the DA of chitin, affecting its overall characteristics (Marzieh MN *et al.,* 2019). The degree of acetylation (DA) significantly influences the applications of chitin, particularly in the food and medical fields. Generally, when the DA is greater than 50%, the substance is classified as chitin, whereas extensive deacetylation results in chitosan. Gbenebor et al. successfully prepared α-chitin from shrimp exoskeleton using NaOH concentrations ranging from 0.4 to 1.2 M, yielding DA values between 99.4% and 74.3%. Similarly, Paul et al. reported that enzymatically extracted chitin from Penaeus monodon had DA values between 80.34% and 82.5%, which were lower than the 84.46% obtained through chemical isolation. Additionally, chitins derived from Metapenaeus monoceros showed DA values of 89.5% and 77%, depending on whether they were prepared via enzymatic deproteinization or alkali treatment. Enzymatically isolated chitins from shrimp (Penaeus kerathurus) and crab were found to have DA values of 88.5% and 78.6%, respectively (Rasweefali, M.K *et al.,* 2022).
Intrinsic viscosity plays a crucial role in the conventional determination of chitin's molecular weight. Generally, a higher molecular weight results in more viscous solutions, although this is not always necessary for commercial applications. The viscosity of chitin in acetic acid tends to increase as pH decreases, whereas in HCl, it decreases with lowering pH, leading to the concept of "intrinsic viscosity." This property is influenced by the degree of ionization and ionic strength. Chitin is considered a high-molecular-weight biopolymer, and its molecular weight varies depending on the source and preparation method. It has been suggested that native chitin often has a molecular weight exceeding one million Daltons. Various factors during chitin production, including high temperature, reaction time, alkali concentration, particle size, acid concentration, and shear stress, can impact its molecular weight (Alabaraoye, E *et al.,* 2018).

Functional Properties Of Chitin

Chitin has a wide range of applications across various industries, including wastewater treatment, food processing, cosmetics, agriculture, pharmaceuticals, medicine, papermaking, and textiles. Its versatility stems from its unique biological, chemical, and physical properties, making it an intriguing material for multiple uses (C., Casadidio *et al.,* 2019). In the biomedical field, chitin offers significant advantages due to its biocompatibility, non-toxic nature, and ability to accelerate wound healing and inhibit tumor cell growth. These properties have driven the development of chitin-based products such as vascular implants, tumor inhibitors, and artificial blood vessels, demonstrating its potential in advanced medical applications (Hassen, T.F *et al.,* 2024).

Chitin is an excellent choice for biomedical applications due to its desirable properties, such as biocompatibility, adhesion, biodegradability, wound-healing capabilities, hemostatic properties, and antibacterial activity (A. M., Sixto-Berrocal *et al.,* 2023). It has been utilized in various forms, including sponges, powders, granules, filaments, and composites with materials like cotton or polyester. Non-woven chitin textiles and strings have been used as synthetic sutures and artificial skin due to their ability to support wound healing. The biochemical mechanisms of chitin in wound healing include fibroblast activation, polymorphonuclear cell activation, stimulation of type IV collagen synthesis, giant cell migration, and cytokine production. Beyond biomedical applications, chitin has gained attention as an effective and cost-efficient adsorbent for toxic metals. Its long polymeric chain structure provides multiple opportunities for modification and derivative production. Chitin, being a high molecular weight polysaccharide, is particularly effective in adsorption-based applications. Polysaccharide-based adsorbents, nanosorbents, and nanomaterials derived from chitin exhibit high efficiency in removing pollutants from water, making it a promising solution for water remediation. The presence of hydroxyl groups in chitin plays a crucial role in governing the kinetics and stereochemistry of chemical reactions, further enhancing its potential for environmental applications (M., Nasrollahzadeh *et al.,* 2021).

Chitin exhibits a broad molecular weight (Mw) range, making it suitable for various applications. In the pharmaceutical industry, chitin-based materials are essential, with low-Mw oligomers being particularly beneficial for wound healing applications, while high-Mw chitin is preferred for tissue engineering (Pakizeh M *et al.,* 2021). Low-Mw chitin extracted from shrimp has demonstrated remarkable anticancer and antiseptic properties, making it highly valuable for drug development. To accurately determine the molecular weight of chitin, it must be completely dissolved in a suitable solvent without undergoing degradation, aggregation, or molecular association. Additionally, fat and water binding capacity (FBC and WBC) are crucial properties influencing chitin's functionality. FBC refers to the amount of oil absorbed per unit weight, whereas WBC reflects chitin's tendency to interact with hydrophilic substances. The sequence of steps in chitin isolation significantly impacts these properties. Studies indicate that conducting demineralization before deproteinization leads to higher WBC and FBC compared to the reverse order, highlighting the importance of process optimization for desired functional properties (Mohan K *et al.,* 2020).

The highly crystalline nature and low solubility of chitin pose significant challenges to its broader application. To address these limitations, numerous studies have explored innovative methods to minimize environmental impact while producing value-added chitin derivatives. One such approach involves enzymatic degradation of pretreated, ground chitin shells to obtain N-acetylglucosamine (GlcNAc) and its dimer $(GlcNAc)_2$, which have applications as skin moisturizers and antimicrobial agents. Additionally, instant catapult steam explosion treatment has been investigated as a means to reduce chitin crystallinity while simultaneously increasing its surface area and pore volume. These structural modifications enhance chitin's potential for dye adsorption by expanding its available binding surface area, making it more effective in environmental applications such as wastewater treatment (Z.Q. Tian *et al.,* 2018).

N-acetylglucosamine (GlcNAc), a polymer derived from chitin, functions as an anti-inflammatory agent. It is naturally synthesized in the human body from glucose and later incorporated into glycoproteins and glycosaminoglycans. When administered, GlcNAc has been shown to be effective in treating conditions such as ulcerative colitis, gastrointestinal disorders, and inflammation. Despite its numerous benefits, the application of chitin is often hindered by its poor solubility, low porosity, and limited surface area. To overcome these challenges and enhance its usability, various significant derivatives of chitin have been developed. Among them, chitosan stands out as one of the most versatile and widely applicable. Chitin derivatives play a crucial role in the production of artificial medical devices, including contact lenses, artificial skin, and surgical sutures. Their extensive use in medical applications is attributed to their non-toxic, non-allergic, biocompatible, and biodegradable properties, making them ideal for biomedical advancements. Rameshthangam et al. (2018) highlight various biomedical applications of chitin and its derivatives. More recently, chitin and its derivatives have also been utilized for the remediation of organic and inorganic contaminants from soil and water. Due to their biocompatibility, they have been employed for immobilizing chitinases, which play a role in detecting hazardous environmental chemicals. Chitin and chitosan are particularly effective in removing dyes, organic pollutants, and heavy metals from the environment. Furthermore, modifications such as functionalization have been explored to enhance chitin's adsorption potential. Techniques include irradiated grafting of acrylonitrile onto chitin, incorporation of polypyrrole, acetophenone derivatives of nanochitosan, cross-linking chitosan into nanohydrogel, and the development of poly-chitin nanofibers. These modifications significantly improve chitin's ability to adsorb heavy metals, making it a promising material for environmental remediation (Singh, R *et al.,* 2021).

Chitin derivatives have well-documented positive effects on human health and play a crucial role in various biological processes. One of chitin's key properties is its high antimicrobial capacity, which primarily functions through cell lysis, leading to the disruption of the target organism's cell membrane. Additionally, chitosan, a major derivative of chitin, has the ability to chelate heavy metals, even in trace amounts. The unique structural properties of chitin allow it to resist degradation by pancreatic juice, bile, and urine, further enhancing its biological stability. Moreover, chitin derivatives demonstrate excellent drug-carrying capabilities, making them highly valuable in clinical applications (Verardi, A *et al.,* 2023). Research on chitin's effects on cardiovascular diseases has also shown promising results, particularly when combined with other bioactive compounds. For instance, chitin, when paired with glucan and pomegranate polyphenols, has been found to counteract endothelial dysfunction. Additionally, chitin combined with graphene oxide in the form of aerogel beads has been shown to effectively absorb excess bilirubin in the blood, highlighting its potential in biomedical and therapeutic applications (Neyrinck AM *et al.,* 2019).

Chitin serves as a moisturizing agent and a film-forming tensor, while both chitin and its derivative, chitosan, act as chelators for metals that are responsible for various contact allergies. Among its derivatives, carboxymethyl chitosan is particularly notable as a multifunctional component in cosmetic formulations. It is non-cytotoxic and is used for its antioxidant, moisture-absorbing, antimicrobial, and stabilizing properties in emulsions. Recently, the concept of cosmeceuticals has gained attention, referring to cosmetic products that not only enhance beauty but also contribute to overall health. Some of these cosmetics, already available on the market, are formulated with chitosan and incorporate pharmaceutical or medicinal properties. These products contain essential oils and active ingredients, including enzymes, antioxidants, vitamins, and phytochemicals, highlighting chitosan's growing role in the cosmetic and skincare industries (Verardi, A *et al.,* 2023).

The functional role of chitin differs across species, serving as either structural support, protection, or both. Chitin and its derivative, chitosan, have gained significant attention in the medical field due to their high biocompatibility. In addition to being biodegradable, chitin also exhibits immunogenicity and mechanical strength, making it highly valuable in biomedical applications. One of its notable properties is its ability to accelerate wound healing by modulating the inflammatory response through interleukin 8, prostaglandin E, and interleukin 1β. This property, along with its versatility in various applications, positions chitin as a promising material for wound dressings. Studies have shown that chitin and chitosan scaffolds are effective in treating severe burns and wounds, further demonstrating their potential in medical treatments (Dave, U *et al.,* 2021). Biopolymers like chitin can be engineered into nanogels, which are hydrogels confined to the nanoscale. These nanogels exhibit remarkable properties, including tunable size, a large surface area for bioconjugation, controlled drug loading and release, and responsiveness to environmental stimuli (Parhi, R *et al.,* 2020). These characteristics have led to innovative applications of chitin in drug delivery, such as water-soluble carboxymethyl chitin (CMC) and polylactic acid (PLA)/chitosan (CS) nanoparticles. Chitin's high surface area, due to its biopolymeric structure, makes it highly effective as a pollutant absorber, facilitating modifications into nanocomposites ideal for environmental applications, such as soil and water pollutant remediation. Its resistance to microbial degradation, strong bonding potential with amino and hydroxyl groups, and affinity for heavy metals allow it to be utilized in detecting and neutralizing environmental hazards (Rameshthangam, P *et al.,* 2018). Additionally, recent studies highlight chitin's essential role in marine ecosystems, where it helps protect coralline algae from the detrimental effects of ocean acidification (Dave, U *et al.,* 2021).

Recent research suggests that modifying chitin into chitin nano-whiskers presents a promising approach for water treatment, owing to the functional groups present in the nanomaterial and its high surface-to-volume ratio (Druzian, S.P *et al.,* 2019). Chitin's natural ability to adsorb dyes has been well studied due to its biopolymeric structure. However, further research is needed to determine whether combining chitin with other compounds could enhance the efficiency of dye removal from solutions. Additionally, the eco-friendly nature of chitin positions it as a viable alternative for coagulants and flocculants in the removal of metal ions from contaminated water systems. Chitin, particularly in its chitosan form, exhibits cationic properties that enable it to alter the medium, facilitating ion-exchange interactions and electrostatic attraction. This characteristic can be harnessed to enhance the dissolution and absorption of heavy metals from solutions, making chitin an effective tool for water purification (Nasrollahzadeh, M *et al.,* 2021).

Chitin plays a crucial role in fungal pathogenicity. While plants do not produce chitin themselves, they secrete enzymes that break down chitin, a key defense mechanism against fungal pathogens. The plant's ability to resist infection relies on the secretion of chitinases, which degrade fungal cell walls and release chitin fragments that trigger plant immune responses. Recognizing this, researchers found that enhancing chitinase expression in plants can significantly improve resistance to fungal infections. Beyond its role in plant immunity, chitin has practical applications in agriculture, particularly in improving soil quality and crop growth. Soil treatment with chitin has been shown to reduce nematode infections in plant roots and enhance resistance to various soil-borne fungal pathogens. Additionally, incorporating chitin into the soil promotes beneficial microbiota changes in the rhizosphere, directly supporting plant development and overall health (Dave, U *et al.,* 2021).

Shrimp Shell And It's Functional Properties

Shrimp can be transformed into various processed products, including frozen, dried, and canned shrimp. Before processing, the shrimp undergo cleaning, during which the head, tail, and shell are removed as waste. This waste is typically regarded as having no economic or practical value and is often discarded or incinerated. However, improper disposal methods can lead to environmental pollution, highlighting the need for sustainable waste management practices (Saputra, D.D *et al.,* 2023).

Shrimp shells contain 42.23% protein, 19.87% crude fiber, 2.89% fat, 13.23% calcium, 2.08% phosphorus, and 9.56% chitin (Mirzah, 2019). Due to this composition, shrimp shells have significant potential for processing into shrimp shell flour, which can be further utilized as a biomaterial for bioplastics and biocoagulants. Shrimp waste flour comes from the shrimp processing industry, primarily consisting of shrimp heads and shells, which account for 30-40% of the total shrimp weight. One major application of shrimp shell waste is the conversion of chitin into chitosan, which serves as a binder for heavy metals in water and can also be used for bioplastic production. Additionally, the protein content in shrimp shells acts as a raw material for bioplastics, while calcium carbonate minerals help enhance the mechanical strength of plastics. However, because shrimp shells are hard and insoluble in water, they require pre-treatment and modification before they can be efficiently processed into biomaterials. In particular, chitin must be converted into a thermoplastic form to serve as a raw material for bioplastics. Shrimp shells contain 30% chitin in their dry matter, but the protein in shrimp shells is tightly bound to chitin and calcium carbonate, forming a protein-chitin-calcium carbonate complex. Therefore, the deproteinization and demineralization processes are crucial to isolate chitin for further applications (Saputra, D.D *et al.,* 2023).

Shrimp shells and viscera contribute significantly to the aroma perception of shrimp dishes due to their distinct volatile compounds (Okabe, Y *et al.,* 2023). These by-products are also valuable sources of bioactive compounds, particularly carotenoprotein, which can be extracted using protease enzymes. The hydrolyzate obtained from carotenoprotein extraction contains 9.4% lipids and 79.6% protein, with a high concentration of essential amino acids (465 mg/g), making it nutritionally rich and beneficial for human consumption (Taghizadeh A *et al.,* 2021). Carotenoprotein also possesses anti-hypertensive and antioxidant (scavenging) properties, making it useful in the food and nutraceutical industries. Additionally, shrimp viscera, particularly from Litopenaeus vannamei, has been purified to obtain heparin-like glycosaminoglycan, a compound with potent anticoagulant and anti-thrombin properties. This compound is also rich in glucuronic acid, which further enhances its pharmaceutical potential (Abuzar *et al.,* 2023).
Crustacean exoskeletons are primarily composed of chitin (15-40%), calcium carbonate (20-50%), and protein (20-40%). The desiccated exoskeletons hold significant economic value, estimated at 100-120 USD per tonne (Deng, J *et al.,* 2020). Shrimp shells (SS), contain valuable bioactive compounds such as astaxanthin, chitin, and protein, which contribute to their commercial importance in various industries. Among these components, chitosan and chitin stand out for their strong antibacterial properties. Chitosan has been extensively utilized as an antimicrobial agent in human health, food safety, and water treatment, showing great potential for water purification and food preservation (Abuzar *et al.,* 2023).

Additionally, shrimp shells exhibit antioxidant properties and contain high levels of EPA (eicosapentaenoic acid) and DHA (docosahexaenoic acid), which are beneficial for human health. The derivatives of shrimp shells, including chitosan, chito-oligomers, and chitin, have broad applications in the pharmaceutical, food, and environmental sectors. Pigmented oil extracted from shrimp residues is recognized for its high antioxidant activity, stability, and affordability. One notable source, Parapenaeus longirostris, contains astaxanthin and carotenoids, which exhibit strong bioactive and antioxidant properties. Astaxanthin is particularly effective in inhibiting lipid peroxidation, stimulating the antioxidant defense system, and modulating inflammatory processes in stressed cells. Astaxanthin extracted from shrimp shells (SS) demonstrates cytotoxic, antioxidant, and anti-tyrosinase properties. It plays a role in tyrosinase inhibition, contributing to its potential in skin health and cosmetic applications. Additionally, astaxanthin is a non-cytotoxic compound found in fibroblasts of the human dermis, making it a safe and effective ingredient in functional foods and skincare products (Chintong *et al.,* 2019).

Astaxanthin is a marine-based ketocarotenoid known for its anti-inflammatory and oxidative stress-reducing properties. Research indicates that it inhibits the growth of breast cancer cells and tumors, reducing their rate of proliferation. Additionally, astaxanthin treatment has shown effectiveness against multiple types of cancer. Similarly, chitosan and chitin extracted from Penaeus monodon have demonstrated anti-cancer properties, particularly against human ovarian cancer cells. However, chitosan exhibited stronger anti-cancer activity compared to chitin. This suggests that chitosan's bioactivity may make it a more promising candidate for cancer treatment applications (Abuzar *et al.,* 2023). Bioactive peptides derived from shrimp waste are high-quality proteins with anti-cancer properties. These peptides have gained attention as natural, cost-effective alternatives to traditional drugs for treating chronic diseases with high mortality rates, including cancer. Their ability to act as functional food ingredients further enhances their potential in health promotion. Additionally, astaxanthin, a lipophilic compound, exhibits potent biological properties, including anti-diabetic, anti-viral, and anti-cancer effects. Its diverse health benefits make it a valuable therapeutic agent and a promising ingredient for functional foods and pharmaceutical applications (Cheikh *et al.,* 2019).

Astaxanthin, a powerful antioxidant, has been shown to have immunomodulatory effects, enhancing the immune system while reducing age-related immunopathology. As the primary carotenoid pigment, astaxanthin possesses bioactive properties that make it valuable in cosmetics, food, and pharmaceuticals. In aquaculture, dietary astaxanthin supplementation has been observed to improve fish growth when fed a high-fat diet, reducing oxidative stress by lowering malondialdehyde levels and increasing superoxide dismutase activity. Additionally, it helped reduce the hepatosomatic index, indicating potential benefits in fish health and metabolism. On the other hand, chitin, the second most abundant biopolymer after cellulose, is highly resistant to degradation and insoluble. However, chitin-derived secondary products have been explored for drug delivery applications and as immune system enhancers in fish, highlighting their potential in biomedical and aquaculture advancements (Abuzar *et al.,* 2023).

Shrimp by-products

Shrimp by-products are valuable sources of nutrients that provide numerous health benefits, including their role in male fertility. Astaxanthin, in particular, has been shown to enhance sperm function and is used to help treat idiopathic infertility in men. As a potent antioxidant, astaxanthin helps reduce oxidative stress, which is crucial for maintaining sperm viability and function. It also plays a protective role against heavy metal toxicity, especially cadmium, which can impair fertility, damage the testes, reduce sperm viability, and increase CatSperl gene expression. Research suggests that astaxanthin supplementation significantly increases sperm count, further supporting its potential in male reproductive health (Saberi *et al.,* 2021).

Shrimp shell (SS) and its derivatives are gaining popularity in the food industry, particularly in functional foods. One notable application is the use of astaxanthin to enhance the flavor of cheese, making it more appealing to consumers. Additionally, oil extracted from shrimp waste serves as a natural ingredient in cheese, margarine, and ice cream, contributing to flavor and stability. In the beverage industry, chitosan is recognized as a potent antimicrobial agent that helps control spoilage microorganisms. While it can damage bacteria and yeast during fermentation, it is still widely used in fermented beverages, particularly wine, due to its effectiveness in preventing spoilage (Guzzon, R *et al.,* 2022). Encapsulated astaxanthin is emerging as a functional ingredient in the food industry, particularly in nutraceuticals. The nutraceutical industry has shown significant interest in shrimp-derived lipids, primarily due to the presence of astaxanthin, DHA, and EPA. These bioactive compounds are being explored to create low-cholesterol, high-PUFA (polyunsaturated fatty acid) products, offering health benefits such as improved cardiovascular health. One approach to making these products even healthier is saponin treatment, which has been found to reduce cholesterol levels (Raju, N *et al.,* 2020). Beyond food applications, shrimp shells (SS) are also utilized as natural preservatives in the pharmaceutical industry due to their antioxidant and scavenging properties. A key component extracted from SS is chitosan, which possesses fat and water-binding properties, making it valuable in food and medical applications. Interestingly, deep-sea chitosan is considered superior to coastal-origin chitosan due to its better structural and commercial properties. This high-quality chitosan has applications in medicine and is known for its anti-cholesterolemic effects, helping to regulate cholesterol levels (Mohammadi, P *et al.,* 2023).

Application Of Chitin To Reduce Toxicity Of Synthetic Food Colors

The increasing use of synthetic food colorants has raised concerns due to their potential health risks, including allergic reactions, hyperactivity, and carcinogenic effects. Synthetic dyes such as Allura Red AC, Tartrazine, and Rhodamine B are widely used in processed foods to enhance their visual appeal but have been linked to toxicological concerns (Oplatowska-Stachowiak & Elliott, 2019). In response, researchers have explored natural biopolymers like chitin and its derivative, chitosan, as potential detoxification agents to mitigate these adverse effects while maintaining food quality and safety.

Allura red AC, also known as "CL Food Red 17", is a synthetic mono-azo red food colouring (E129) with the chemical formula C18H14N2Na2O8S2. This additive is used in decorations and coatings for pastry products, confectionery including breath refreshing and chewing gum, pastry and fine bakery products, flavoured fermented milk products, edible cheese rinds, desserts, preserves of fruits, ice cream, flavoured drinks, baked crustaceans, seafood, breakfast sausages, appetizers, sauces, seasonings, soups, luncheon meat, replacements, and alcoholic beverages. It can be delivered as a sodium, calcium, or potassium salt (Silva *et al.,* 2022). AR consumption has been related to occasional behavioral alterations in humans and animals, including increased hyperactivity in children, although further studies are needed (Noorafshan *et al.,* 2018). Regarding possible side effects on health, it has been reported that E129 is an allergizing substance which worsens or induces asthma, rhinitis, or hives [18]. There is also the possibility of the presence of carcinogenic residues in this food colouring, and it is suspected of hyperkinesia. The EFSA has advised an ADI of 7.0 mg/kg bw/day (Al-Shabib *et al.,* 2019).

Chitin is a naturally occurring polysaccharide found in the exoskeletons of crustaceans, insects, and fungal cell walls. Due to its high adsorption capacity, it has been investigated for its ability to bind and neutralize harmful compounds, including heavy metals, mycotoxins, and synthetic dyes in food systems (Younes & Rinaudo, 2021). Studies have demonstrated that chitosan, a deacetylated derivative of chitin, interacts with synthetic dyes through electrostatic attraction, hydrogen bonding, and Van der Waals forces, leading to effective removal or neutralization of these compounds (Dutta *et al.,* 2021).

Recent advancements in food safety technology have led to the development of chitin-based adsorbents, membranes, and biofilms that selectively capture synthetic dyes while preserving the overall quality of food products (Muzzarelli *et al.,* 2019). In addition to its detoxification properties, chitin has exhibited antioxidant and antimicrobial effects, further enhancing its potential as a functional food ingredient (Suresh *et al.,* 2020). The use of chitin-based nano-filtration systems has been explored to remove food color contaminants from beverages and processed foods, ensuring compliance with food safety regulations (López-Maldonado *et al.,* 2018).

The role of chitin in detoxification extends beyond food processing. Biomedical applications have demonstrated its ability to bind to toxicants in the gastrointestinal tract, preventing their absorption into the bloodstream (Ali & Ahmed, 2018). Similar mechanisms are being explored for chitin-coated packaging materials, which could help reduce synthetic dye migration into food products during storage and transportation (Rinaudo, 2019).

Globally, there is a growing demand for safer, eco-friendly alternatives to chemical detoxification methods. Chitin-based solutions provide a sustainable approach to reducing the risks associated with synthetic food dyes, aligning with the increasing consumer preference for clean-label products (Madhavi & Kagan, 2021). However, challenges remain in terms of scalability, regulatory approval, and cost-effectiveness, necessitating further research into optimizing chitin extraction, processing, and application in food safety (Sharma *et al.,* 2023).

Despite these challenges, the incorporation of chitin in food safety applications represents a promising avenue for mitigating the toxicity of synthetic food colorants. Future research should focus on refining chitin-based detoxification strategies, enhancing their efficiency, and exploring their potential integration into mainstream food processing technologies (Kumar *et al.,* 2022).

Several studies have demonstrated that chitin and chitosan interact with synthetic food dyes through adsorption, ion exchange, and complexation mechanisms. The amine ($-NH_2$) and hydroxyl (-OH) groups present in chitosan enable it to bind negatively charged dye molecules, leading to their removal from aqueous solutions (Dutta *et al.,* 2020). Research has shown that: Chitosan can effectively adsorb anionic dyes such as Allura Red and Tartrazine, reducing their bioavailability in the digestive system (Ali & Ahmed, 2018), Chitin-based biofilms have been developed to filter out synthetic dyes from processed food products while maintaining color stability (López-Maldonado *et al.,* 2016), Chitosan nano-adsorbents have exhibited a high removal efficiency for azo dyes, indicating potential for food detoxification applications (Sharma *et al.,* 2023).

Beyond direct detoxification, chitin and its derivatives have been incorporated into active food packaging materials to reduce dye migration and contamination. Chitosan-coated films have been shown to act as protective barriers against synthetic dye leaching in processed foods such as soft drinks, candies, and sauces (Rinaudo, 2021). Moreover, these coatings provide antimicrobial protection, extending the shelf life of food products while simultaneously reducing exposure to harmful dyes (Suresh *et al.,* 2020). In biomedical research, chitin and chitosan have been explored for their ability to bind toxic substances in the gastrointestinal tract, suggesting that dietary supplementation with chitin-based materials may help mitigate dye-related toxicity (Madhavi & Kagan, 2021). Chitosan-based dietary supplements may prevent the absorption of synthetic dyes into the bloodstream (Ali & Ahmed, 2018). Chitin-fortified food products could serve as functional ingredients to counteract oxidative damage caused by synthetic colorants (Kumar *et al.,* 2022). Chitosan nanoparticles have potential applications in enzyme-assisted detoxification processes, aiding in the breakdown of synthetic dyes before they reach systemic circulation (Sharma *et al.,* 2023).

Conclusion

Chitin, a ubiquitous biopolymer second only to cellulose, exhibits a fascinating interplay between its structural characteristics and diverse functional properties. Its inherent insolubility, stemming from a robust hydrogen bonding network, has historically posed challenges for detection and processing. However, understanding its chemical composition, semi-crystalline nature, and the existence of distinct polymorphic forms (α, β, and γ) is crucial for unlocking its potential. While traditional methods for chitin analysis often involved harsh chemical treatments, advancements in modern structural, spectroscopic, and chromatographic techniques have significantly improved our ability to characterize and quantify this biopolymer. The ability to manipulate chitin's structure through deacetylation to chitosan further expands its versatility. Ultimately, a comprehensive understanding of chitin's structural intricacies is fundamental for harnessing its wide-ranging applications in diverse fields, including industry, food science, biomedicine, and environmental sustainability. Continued research into efficient extraction, dissolution, and modification methods will be key to fully exploiting the remarkable structural and functional properties of chitin.

Reference

1. Bradić, A., Zemljič, L. F., & Knez, Ž. (2020). Extraction and characterization of chitin and chitosan from different sources. *Marine Drugs*, *18*(12), 624.
2. El Knidri, H., Brahimi Errahmani, M., Benhaddou, R., & Vignon, M. R. (2020). Physicochemical characterization of chitin and chitosan extracted from *Sepia officinalis* cuttlebone. *International Journal of Biological Macromolecules*, *150*, 773-783.
3. Hahn, T., Tiefenbacher, P., & Struck, U. (2020). Revealing the distribution of chitin polymorphs in fungal cell walls by solid-state NMR spectroscopy. *Biomacromolecules*, *21*(1), 335-345.
4. Ifuku, S., Nogi, M., Abe, H., Hongo, T., Yano, H., & Miyamoto, Y. (2009). Transparent and high gas barrier films based on nanostructured chitin. *Biomacromolecules*, *10*(6), 1584-1591.
5. Knidri, H. E., Laajeb, A., El Rhilassi, A., Benhaddou, R., & Vignon, M. R. (2018). Extraction, chemical modification and characterization of chitin and chitosan from *Parapenaeus longirostris* shrimp waste. *Process Biochemistry*, *66*, 110-118.
6. Ling, S., Harding, S. E., & Stokes, J. R. (2018). Chitin structure, physicochemical properties and biofunctional applications. *Carbohydrate Polymers*, *184*, 286-299.
7. Lopes, R. P., Reis, R. L., & Mano, J. F. (2018). Chitin and chitosan for tissue engineering and regenerative medicine applications. *Progress in Polymer Science*, *86*, 1-39.
8. Muzzarelli, R. A. A. (2011). Chitin nanofibrils and nanofibers as versatile biomaterials. *Marine Drugs*, *9*(11), 2068-2087.
9. Tsurkan, M. V., Ceseracciu, L., Pignatelli, F., Nanni, P., Tyuftin, A. I., & Heredia-Guerrero, J. A. (2020). A critical review on the physicochemical and biological properties of chitin and its derivatives. *Molecules*, *25*(19), 4423.
10. Wang, J., Chen, H., Shao, W., & Chen, X. (2021). Facile and green dissolution of α-chitin in NaOH/urea aqueous solution at low temperature. *International Journal of Biological Macromolecules*, *183*, 1217-1225.

CHAPTER 5

FUNCTIONAL PROPERTIES OF PHYTOSTEROL

Subha S
Department of Food Science and Nutrition, Nehru Arts and Science College, Coimbatore, Tamil Nadu-641 105

INTRODUCTION

Phytosterols are naturally occurring substances originating from plants that are widely dispersed in plants and have a chemical structure and physiological function comparable to cholesterol. A glycosidic or ester link can covalently connect phytosterols or split them into their free form. The structural differences of phytosterols are directly associated with their bioactivities. Phytosterols have attracted a lot of attention lately due to their remarkable physiological action. Among the many physiological benefits of phytosterols are their ability to reduce cholesterol, reduce inflammation, and prevent cancer. Over time, eating foods high in phytosterols can reduce the risk of cancer by 20%. Moreover, phytosterols have been found to be quite effective at preventing cardiovascular and cerebrovascular diseases in humans.Since people cannot create phytosterols on their own, they are mostly found in nuts, mushrooms, and vegetable oils. Between 150 to 400 mg of total sterols, mostly in the form of β-sitosterol, campesterol, and soy sterols, are reported to be present in our daily diet. Human serum phytosterol levels vary from 2.9 to 17.0 mg/L, indicating a very low intestine absorption rate for phytosterols. A little increase in daily phytosterol intake has been demonstrated to improve human health; 2 g of phytosterols daily has been shown to reduce low-density lipoprotein cholesterol levels by 7–10%.(Shen *et al.,* 2024)

More than 250 PSs have been isolated, and the phytosterol concentration varies per plant type. Numerous studies have shown that PSs have remarkable pharmacological advantages as chemopreventive, anti-inflammatory, antioxidant, antidiabetic, and antiatherosclerotic agents. However, a variety of factors, including as type, source, processing, preparation, delivery route, food matrix, dosage, time of administration into the body, and genetic factors, might alter PS bioavailability, which is a serious problem. Low absorption rates have also been said to be closely associated with their chemical structures, including side-chain length and saturation degree. Therefore, this study aims to provide thorough information on PS's therapeutic potential for human health, with an emphasis on preclinical effects and issues linked to bioavailability.(Shen *et al.,* 2024)

These days, one potential strategy to improve health is to use natural substances in food to regulate physiological functions. As one of the recommended dietary components, the health benefits of phytosterols—naturally occurring bioactive compounds found in plants—have gained increased attention. Scientists are very interested in phytosterols because of their many physiological qualities, which include their capacity to lower cholesterol, prevent cancer, lessen inflammation, and affect the immune system.(Shen *et al.,* 2024)

Dietary intake of natural substances to regulate physiological functions is currently regarded as a potential way of promoting health. As one of the recommended dietary ingredients, phytosterols that are natural bioactive compounds distributed in plants have received increasing attention for their health effects. Phytosterols have attracted great attention from scientists because of many physiological functions, for example, cholesterol-lowering, anticancer, anti-inflammatory, and immunomodulatory effects. In addition, the physiological functions of phytosterols, the purification, structure analysis, synthesis, and food application of phytosterols have been widely studied. Nowadays, many bioactivities of phytosterols have been assessed in vivo and in vitro.(Lanlan Yuan *et al.,*2024)

Phytosterols (PSs), classified into plant sterols and stanols, are bioactive compounds found in foods of plant origin. PSs have been proposed to exert a wide number of pharmacological properties, including the potential to reduce total and low-density lipoprotein (LDL) cholesterol levels and thereby decreasing the risk of cardiovascular diseases. Other health-promoting effects of PSs include anti-obesity, anti-diabetic, anti-microbial, anti-inflammatory, and immunomodulatory effects. Also, anticancer effects have been strongly suggested, as phytosterol-rich diets may reduce the risk of cancer by 20%. The aim of this review is to provide a general overview of the available evidence regarding the beneficial physiological and pharmacological activities of PSs, with special emphasis on their therapeutic potential for human health and safety.(Elyas Nattagh-Eshtivani *et al.,*2021)

MECHANISM OF ACTION:

The phytosterol mechanism is similar ti cholesterol.Bile acids, PSs, and billary cholesterol are among the dietary fats that are soluble in micelles. PSs enter enterocytes through either passive diffusion or a receptor-mediated mechanism when pancreatic ester hydroxylase is present. While the trans-membrane transport protein Niemann-Pick C1-Like 1 (NPC1L1) absorbs free PSs and cholesterols, other lipids enter the enterocytes by enhanced diffusion at the brush boundary. ATP-binding cassette co-transporters G5 and G8 (ABCG5/ABCG8) are efflux transporters that export free sterols and unesterified cholesterols back into the lumen after entering the enterocyte. However, PSs are secreted at a significantly higher rate than cholesterol, which explains why plant sterols are less effective at being absorbed than cholesterol.The ATP-binding cassette transporter 2 (ACAT2) then esterifies some free PSs that evade clearance mechanisms and combine with dietary and billary cholesterols to form chylomicrons. Additionally, ATP-binding cassette transporters A1 (ABC A1) have the ability to carry free PSs and attach them to high-density lipoprotein (HDL) particles in enterocytes' basolateral membrane. PSs are released into the bloodstream as part of very-low-density lipoprotein (VLDL) particles after the chylomicron remnants have passed through the liver. Lipoproteins have varying ratios of PSs and esterified cholesterols. Low-density lipoprotein (LDL) and VLDL have the same proportion, whereas HDL, which has a higher PS/cholesterol ratio, does not. Additionally, PSs are broken down by a number of enzymes before being released into bile by the hepatic ABC G5 and G8 transporters. Because they are 2.8–27.9 pmol/L and 4.25–6.5 mmol/L, respectively, the average plasma levels of PSs represent around 0.5% of the entire value of plasma cholesterol concentrations. (Hanieh Barghchi *et al.*,2021)

Table - 1 Phytosterol food sources and their content

PHYTOSTEROLFOOD SOURCES	PHYTOSTEROL'S CONTENT (mg/kg of Fresh weight)
OILS	
Corn	7150-9520
Olive	1140-1150
Palm	490-610
Peanut	1670-2290
Rice bran	10550
Soy Bean	2210-3280
Sunflower	2030-3280
VEGETABLES	
Broccoli	367-390
Carrot	153-160
Cauliflower	310-400
Onion	84-93
Potato	38-73
Tomato	47-148
FRUITS	
Apple	130-183
Banana	116-161
Grapes	40-200
Orange	228-240
NUTS	
Almond	1380-1430
Peanuts	600-1608

CEREALS	
Barely	720-801
Buckwheat	963-1980
Corn	662-1205
Oats	350-491
Rye	707-1130
Wheat	447-830

Source: Tolve et al., 2020

MAJOR CLASSIFICATIONOF PHYTOSTEROLS:

A subclass of steroids, phytosterols are a significant family of bioorganic molecules found in a wide variety of plants, animals, marine life, and fungus. Their structures are similar to those of cholesterol. These substances have long been used as food or medicine, and they are widely accepted to be safe and free of unfavorable side effects. Beta-sitosterol, campesterol, and stigmasterol are the three main categories into which phytosterols fall.

A. STIGMASTEROL:

Stigmasterol is one of the most common plant sterols and is present in many natural sources, including vegetable fats and oils made from a variety of plants. Currently, molecular docking and in vitro and in vivo investigations have been used to study the varied biological impacts of stigmasterol on a variety of metabolic illnesses. Anti-inflammatory, anti-diabetic, immunomodulatory, antiparasitic, antifungal, antibacterial, antioxidant, neuroprotective, anticancer, and anti-osteoarthritis properties are among the potent pharmacological effects demonstrated by the data. In reality, stigmasterol, which is present in plants and algae, is a promising molecule in the development of cancer treatment drugs because it triggers intracellular signaling pathways in a variety of cancers. Stigmasterol and sorafenib together enhanced caspase-3 activation and reduced Bcl-2, an anti-apoptotic protein, in breast cancer.Antioxidant activities that ensure lipid peroxidation and DNA damage reduction are responsible for stigmasterol's chemoprotective qualities in skin cancer. The neuroprotective effects of stigmasterol are also impacted by the control of reactive oxygen species (ROS), in addition to dopamine depletion and acetylcholinesterase inhibition. The anti-inflammatory properties of phytosterols result in the inhibition of cyclooxygenase-2 (COX-2) and inducible nitric oxide synthase (iNOS), the reduction of inflammatory mediator release, and the production of anti-inflammatory cytokines. Stigmasterol has anti-diabetic effects via reducing fasting glucose, blood insulin levels, and oral glucose tolerance. Soybean, rapeseed, and Calabar bean oils are among the many foods that contain stigmasterol, a phytosterol. Additionally, some medicinal plants, including Ficus hirta, Croton sublyratus, Epista prostrate, Epista alba (L.) Hassk, Eucalyptus globules, Akebia quinata, Desmodium styracifolium, Gypsophila oldhamiana, Parkia speciosa, Emilia sonchifolia, Aralia cordata, and Heracleum rapula, have been found to contain it.(Bakrim *et al.,* 2022)

BIOLOGICAL FUNCTIONS :

Anti-inflammatory effects, anti-osteoarthritis effects, and anticancer properties The activities of stigmasterol include immunomodulatory effects, neuroprotective effects, antibacterial activity, antifungal activity, antioxidant activity, anti-diabetic effects, antiparasitic activity, and antiviral activity.(Bakrim *et al.,* 2022)

A phytosterol obtained from a variety of herbaceous plants, including tobacco, soybeans, and herbs, stigmasterol has drawn a lot of interest due to its several pharmacological properties, which include reducing blood cholesterol, preventing inflammation, and preventing diabetes. Stigmasterol has become a prospective therapy option for malignant tumors because of its potent anti-tumor bioactivity. Because it promotes apoptosis, inhibits tumor cell proliferation, invasion, and metastasis, and triggers autophagy, stigmasterol is thought to have an anti-tumor efct on a variety of malignancies, including those of the breast, lung, liver, and ovaries.(X. Zhang *et al.,* 2022)

B. BETA –SITOSTEROL:

One important family of bioorganic compounds are phytosterols, which are steroidal subclasses. A subclass of steroids, phytosterols are an important family of bioorganic substances. It is known that phytosterols, which are present in a wide variety of organisms, including plants, fungi, and mammals, structurally resemble cholesterol. This phytosterol is found naturally in plant cell membranes. It shares a chemical structure with cholesterol derived from mammalian cells and appears to have anti-inflammatory properties. One phytosterol that has been shown to have anti-inflammatory qualities is β-sitosterol. Plant foods high in lipids, such as legumes, nuts, seeds, and extra-virgin olive oil, are especially rich in these molecules. Sterols like sitosterol, stigmasterol, and campesterol are crucial phytosterols to take into account while discussing the development of herbal nutrition for humans.(Khan *et al.,* 2022)

Biological functions:

a. ANTI-CANCER:

Beta- sitosterol sterols decreases the progression and spread of cancer cells, as well as the occurrence of the colon, breast, and prostate cancer in animals exposed to various carcinogens. There is currently evidence that β-sitosterol (2.4–32 M or more) can inhibit the growth of cancer cells and even kill them. Prostate, breast, liver, colon, and mouse fibrosarcoma cells all contain it. Consuming phytosterols is highly associated with a lower risk of stomach cancer in adults, despite the lack of research on their effect on stomach cancer. The effects of β-sitosterol on ceramide metabolism, the activation of caspase-3 and the Fast-signaling mechanism, the increase in pro-apoptotic Bax protein expression, the restoration of gap junctional intercellular communication (GJIC), and changes in the cell cycle dynamics to specific cancer cells. β-sitosterol causes cellular death and has an influence on the proliferative effect of cells. Information about β-sitosterol's effect on stomach cancer is lacking. In Asia, stomach cancer is one of the leading causes of mortality.(Khan *et al.,* 2022)

b. ANTI-INFLAMMATION:

β-sitosterol, the most prevalent phytosterol in plants, has a variety of anti-inflammatory and anti-tumor properties that help prevent a number of chronic illnesses.Diseases such as chronic liver disease, which are clinically indistinguishable from other illnesses, cause a significant amount of morbidity and mortality worldwide. Acute and chronic ethanol intake, aflatoxins in food, viral infections such as hepatitis C and B (including HCV), nonalcoholic fatty liver disease (NAFLD), and other sporadic disorders such hemochromatosis and autoimmune hepatitis are some of the causes of liver disease. Persistent tissue injury typically causes the body to respond with a permanent scarring reaction, which gradually changes the liver's shape and function and leads to cirrhosis and HCC. It includes anti-inflammatory, anti-diabetic, antiviral, and lipid homeostasis modification.(Khan *et al.,* 2022)

C. CAMPESTEROL:

Campesterol, a plant sterol in nature, is known to have cholesterol lowering and anticarcinogenic effects.It was predicted that this compound's anticancer effects would involve an antiangiogenic action because angiogenesis is essential for cancer. Campesterol is one of the most common plant sterols in nature, along with stigmasterol and ß-sitosterol. Large amounts of campesterol can be found in seeds, nuts, grains, beans, legumes, and vegetable oils. It is structurally similar to cholesterol and is metabolized by gut bacteria similarly. Because of their structural similarity to cholesterol, plant sterols, such campesterol, can lower cholesterol. Other biological characteristics of plant sterols include antifungal, antibacterial, anti-inflammatory, and anticarcinogenic actions. It has been demonstrated that campesterol possesses chemopreventive properties against a number of cancers, including prostate, lung, and breast cancers.(Choi *et al.,* 2017)

Biological functions:

a. Cholesterol-Lowering Effects:

Lower blood cholesterol levels result from campesterol's competition with dietary cholesterol for intestinal absorption. Preventing cardiovascular illnesses is a benefit of this.

b. Immune Modulation:

It may influence immune responses and has been studied for its potential to reduce symptoms of autoimmune diseases.

c. Antioxidant Activity:

Campesterol possesses antioxidant properties, protecting cells from oxidative stress and reducing inflammation..(Choi *et al.,* 2017)

APPLICATION OF PHYTOSTEROLS:

A. Applications in functional foods:

Nutraceuticals, functional foods, and natural antioxidants are all made with phytosterols. They can be added to biscuits, serve as fat alternatives, and reduce cholesterol. To treat hypercholesterolemia, a unique free-phytosterol premix was created. Additionally, a light cream cheese spread containing 6 g of phytosterols/100 g (LGC6) was created by researchers. Compared to cheese spread without phytosterols, LGC6 is a functional meal that has the ability to reduce LDL cholesterol and has more elastic qualities. For soft and creamy foods like margarine or spreads, crambe oils (CRs) were used to create nanostructured lipid carriers (NLCs) that can carry free phytosterols. Because of their high biological activity, phytosterols may find use in medications and food additives. They have been shown to have anti-inflammatory, anti-cancer, and cholesterol-lowering properties.Because of their high biological activity, phytosterols may find use in medications and food additives. They have been shown to have anti-inflammatory, anti-cancer, and cholesterol-lowering properties. Adding phytosterols to functional sweeteners may make them more well-liked. Phytosterols have also been utilized to enhance stimuli-responsive qualities in transdermal medication delivery systems. Because of their great surface activity and durable emulsification, phytosterols—particularly β-sitosterol—can be employed in skincare products to substitute cholesterol in the cosmetics sector. Furthermore, because of their many biological functions in animals, phytosterols have a wide range of potential uses in the feed industry and could be used as a novel functional feed additive.(Shen *et al.,* 2024)

PHYSIOLOGICAL FUNCTION OF PHYTOSTEROLS:

A. Anticancer Effects:

Consuming phytosterols may lower your risk of developing breast, stomach, colon, and ovarian cancers, according to recent research. According to meta-analyses, a moderate daily intake of phytosterols (>200 mg) may hinder the growth of tumors by decreasing cancer hallmarks and blocking oncogenic signaling. Phytosterols have been shown to have a number of anticancer properties, including preventing the generation of carcinogens, reducing the growth of cancer cells, triggering apoptosis, and preventing angiogenesis. Campesterol, for instance, has antiangiogenic qualities, but β-sitosterol may prevent tumor growth by blocking the sphingomyelin cycle and protein kinase C (PKC) pathways. It may also activate ceramide and protein phosphatase 2A (PP2A) to encourage cell death.(Shen *et al.,* 2024)

B. Antioxidation Activities:

Especially β-sitosterol, phytosterols have strong antioxidant properties. They use radical adduct formation (RAF) or hydrogen transfer (HT) processes to scavenge free radicals. Phytosterols alleviate oxidative stress by lowering peroxide levels, increasing the activity of antioxidant enzymes (such as SOD, CAT, and GPx), and directly neutralizing reactive oxygen species (ROS). By enhancing ATP synthesis and mitochondrial membrane potential, phytosterols also shield mitochondria from oxidative stress, preventing damage to the respiratory complex and mitochondrial DNA. To prevent oxidative stress, β-sitosterol, for instance, can cause mitochondrial uncoupling, which lowers damage and improves glutathione redox cycling.(Shen *et al.,* 2024)

C. Cholesterol-Lowering Effects

Animal cell membranes depend on cholesterol, but abnormalities in its management can result in diseases like diabetes, heart disease, and neurological disorders. There are two primary types of cholesterol: endogenous (made by the liver) and exogenous (found in food). While the liver controls cholesterol levels through receptors like LDLR, proteins like NPC1L1 control the absorption of cholesterol from the intestines. It has been demonstrated that phytosterols, which are compounds derived from plants, reduce cholesterol through a number of mechanisms. These include replacing cholesterol in intestinal micelles, which decreases absorption; influencing the expression of transport proteins, such as NPC1L1 and ABCG5/8, which promotes cholesterol excretion; interfering with the formation of chylomicrons; and upregulating LDLR expression, which increases cholesterol clearance.Additionally, phytosterols can inhibit enzymes involved in cholesterol synthesis, such as HMG-CoA reductase, further contributing to cholesterol reduction. Their cholesterol-lowering effects vary based on their structure, with phytosterol esters proving more effective than free phytosterols in reducing cholesterol levels and atherosclerosis risk.(Shen *et al.,* 2024)

D. Immunomodulatory Effects:

T-cell proliferation and natural killer cell activity have been shown to be enhanced by phytosterols, especially β-sitosterol, which has immunomodulatory effects. Research indicates that β-sitosterol has the ability to modify the T-helper immune response and change T-helper (Th1) cytokine profiles. For example, it increases peripheral blood mononuclear cell counts, stimulates pig dendritic cells, and improves vaccine responses to the porcine reproductive and respiratory syndrome virus. Additionally, phytosterols affect T-cell populations (such as CD3+, CD4+, and CD8+) and control immune-related genes, like sterol regulatory element-binding proteins (SREBP), which aid in lowering viral replication in CD8+ cells. Furthermore, β-sitosterol has been utilized in aquaculture to boost fish immunity and increases phagocytic activity.(Shen *et al.,* 2024)

E. Anti-Inflammatory Effects:

Numerous illnesses, including obesity, arthritis, and cardiovascular disease, are associated with inflammation. Research has indicated that phytosterols, including β-sitosterol, stigmasterol, and campesterol, have anti-inflammatory properties. They might work by altering important signaling pathways that are implicated in inflammatory reactions, like MAPK and NF-κB. Phytosterols have the ability to modulate MAPK pathways that affect the expression of cytokines and block the activation of NF-κB, which governs the creation of inflammatory mediators. Phytosterols may also affect cell polarization, which would lower the activation of M1 proinflammatory macrophages. According to certain research, phytosterols enhance anti-inflammatory responses by activating liver X receptors (LXRs). However, structural elements like the location of the double bond and steric characteristics may affect how effective they are.(Shen *et al.,* 2024)

F. Other Physiological Functions

Red seaweed (Laurencia papillosa) contains phytosterols that have antibacterial properties against Gram-negative bacteria. They also control the pathways involved in energy metabolism and the composition of the gut microbiome. In addition to these benefits, phytosterols have hormone-like, cholesterol-lowering, and antidiabetic actions. The brain depends on cholesterol homeostasis, and neurological problems can result from abnormalities in cholesterol metabolism. According to research, β-sitosterol, stigmasterol, and other sterols including brassicasterol and lanosterol may be able to control neurodegenerative illnesses in vivo as well as in vitro.(Shen *et al.,* 2024)

CONCLUSION

Phytosterols, structurally similar to cholesterol, exhibit a range of functional properties that hold significant promise for human health. Their well-established cholesterol-lowering effects, achieved through competitive inhibition of intestinal cholesterol absorption, position them as valuable dietary interventions for cardiovascular disease prevention. Beyond this primary function, emerging research highlights their potential antioxidant, anti-inflammatory, and even anti-cancer activities, suggesting a broader role in promoting overall well-being.The incorporation of phytosterols into functional foods and supplements has expanded their accessibility, offering consumers a proactive approach to managing cholesterol levels and potentially benefiting from their other bioactive properties. However, factors such as the specific type and dosage of phytosterol, as well as individual physiological responses, can influence their efficacy. Future research should focus on elucidating the precise mechanisms underlying their diverse effects, optimizing delivery methods, and exploring potential synergistic interactions with other dietary components. Overall, the functional properties of phytosterols underscore their importance as valuable bioactives in the pursuit of improved health and disease prevention.

REFERENCE

1. Achinna, P. (2011). Phytosterol - a Functional Ingredient for Indian Food Industry. *Indian Food Industry*, *30*(3), 35-38.
2. Nigam, M., et al. (2023). Phytosterols: From Preclinical Evidence to Potential Clinical Applications. *Antioxidants*, *12*(2), 334.
3. Rathinapriya, P., et al. (2021). Phytosterols in Seaweeds: An Overview on Biosynthesis to Biomedical Applications. *Marine Drugs*, *22*(23), 12691.
4. Tomer, N., et al. (2024). Novel phytosterol with Antimicrobial Potential of *Digera muricata* Mart. from Chittorgarh Region, India. *Journal of Pure and Applied Microbiology*, *18*(3), 1648-1660.
5. Jayaraman, S., et al. (2021). An Overview on the Therapeutic Function of Foods Enriched with Plant Sterols in Diabetes Management. *Foods*, *10*(12), 3068.
6. Patel, P. K., Sarma, R., Gogoi, B., Singh, S. K., Handique, N., & Babu, A. (2023). Phytosterol Composition in the Oil of Bi-clonal Seed Stocks of Tea (*Camellia sinensis* L.) in North East India. *Journal of Plantation Crops*, *51*(3), 128–132.
7. Kumar, M. S. S., Geetha, K. S., Chandrasekar, K., Govindan, R., Kumar, P. M., Mahendra, J., & Rajagopal, P. (2023). Phytosterols and its neuroprotective effect – an updated review. *European Chemical Bulletin*, *12*(Special Issue 4), 7816-7832.
8. Kumar, M. S. S., Ali, K., Dahuja, A., & Tyagi, A. (2015). Role of phytosterols in drought stress tolerance in rice. *Plant Physiology and Biochemistry*, *96*, 83-89.
9. Nagayach, S. (2015). PHYTOSTEROLS AND THE HEALTH. *Medico Research Chronicles*, *2*(3), 260-263.
10. Kuna, A., & Achinna, P. (2011). Phytosterol - a Functional Ingredient for Indian Food Industry. *Indian Food Industry*, *30*(3), 35-38

CHAPTER 6

FUNCTIONAL PROPERTIES OF CASTOR (RICINUS COMMUNIS) SEED

Fabina K

Department of Food Science and Nutrition, Nehru Arts and Science College, Coimbatore, Tamil Nadu-641 105

INTRODUCTION

One of the oldest and most important non-edible oilseed crops is castor, or Ricinus communis L. It is a significant member of the medicinal plant family Euphorbiaceae. This chapter assesses the ethnomedical use of castor, its phytochemistry, and its biological and pharmacological action. Flavonoids, phenolic compounds, fatty acids, amino acids, terpenoids, phytosterol, and other chemical components are all present in castor. These compounds have been shown to have anti-inflammatory, antibacterial, antioxidant, hepatoprotective, insecticidal, anticonception, antidiabetic, antifertility, and wound-healing qualities. Castor has also shown repelling properties and the ability to scavenge free radicals and mercury.While the leaves can be used to treat burns, biliousness, antiviral, ear and headache issues, night blindness, and malaria, the stem can be used to treat hypoglycemia and cancer. The flowers can be used to relieve vaginal and glandular pain. Fruits are used to cure cancer as well as disorders of the liver, spleen, and piles. As a purgative, root can be used to treat rheumatoid arthritis, ascites, leprosy, rectal pains, hypoglycemia, asthma, and bronchitis. Because it includes the extremely toxic proteins ricin and ricinine, the castor oil plant has also demonstrated adverse consequences. However, further research is still required to determine its medical value and the active ingredients that give it its many different properties.(jasminkumar kheni *et al.,*2023)

Between 40 and 60 percent of the seeds are oil. Because it is the only commercial source of a hydroxylated fatty acid, its oil is distinct from other vegetable oils. The deadly protein ricin, together with other toxic components including ricinine and ricinoleic acids, renders the castor seed inedible. Castor seed intake has been seriously hampered by the presence of poisonous components in the seeds. With differing degrees of efficacy and restrictions, different detoxification techniques have been employed. According to reports, 51% of raw castor seeds are carbohydrates, 6.02% are ash, 6.65% are fat, and 6.62% are fiber. Animal feed made from castor husk and meal: Detoxified castor meal is suitable for use as feed.With no negative effects, broiler finishing diets might include up to 100gkg-1 of castor meal that has been detoxified by boiling. Numerous cellular, metabolic, and chemical changes, such as chromosome abnormalities and DNA damage, decreased RNA and protein synthesis, modifications to enzymes and food stores, and loss of membrane integrity, are linked to seed deterioration. Lipids, carbohydrates, proteins, and, of course, nucleic acids are the main components of seeds. However, different species' seeds have different amounts of each component. While some seeds are high in carbs, others are high in lipids, proteins, or both.(BO Apuyor *et al.,*2022)

The castor plant, Ricinus communis, belonging to the Euphorbiaceous family, has drawn the attention of researchers since it is inedible and renewable. In several industrial processes, it serves as a raw material. The Euphorbiaceous family includes the perineal oil crop seed Ricinus communis, which is grown in warm temperate regions. About 0.15% of the world's vegetable oil is produced from Ricinus communis, an old and extensively cultivated crop in the spurge family. Ricinoleic acid, an 18-carbon monounsaturated fatty acid, makes up 90% of castor oil. It has an acid group at the first carbon, a double bond between the ninth and tenth carbons, and a hydroxyl functional group at the twelfth carbon.(ZI Mkhize *et al.,*2023)

In the areas of polymers, pharmaceuticals, biodiesel production, lubricants, and cosmetics, there are over 700 applications. The oil content of castor seeds ranged from 30% to 50%. In general, varying extraction methods can extract anywhere from 30% to 35% of the oil from various plant fruits and seeds. To increase the efficacy of conventional solvent extraction, however, a lot of emphasis has been paid to the quest for a better extraction method. The classic solvent extraction procedure often takes over an hour to complete and consumes a lot of energy, depending on the solvent rates of diffusion.(Nur Atirah Ibrahim *et al.,*2018)

The important oilseed crop Ricinus communis is often used in traditional cultures due to its medicinal properties. Many ailments, including as rhinitis, bronchitis, dental caries, scabies, skin disorders, and digestive tract infections, are treated using the plant's extracts. Few studies have described the chemical variety of these extracts using advanced chemical profiling techniques, despite all of their medicinal advantages.(Perla M Santos *et al.,*2018)

The oil from castor beans (Ricinus communis L.) is highly valued, and the composition of the oil's fatty acids directly affects the oil's quality. As a result, producing oil in vitro with desired fatty acid profiles is an exciting area of study that may also provide commercial prospects.(Zeynep Ergun *et al.,*2022)

HEALTH BENEFITS OF CASTOR SEED:

a. Antibacterial activity

The activity of R. communis has been examined using a range of aqueous and solvent-based extracts. Butanolic, ethyl acetate, methanolic, and hot and cold ethanolic extracts are some of the several solvent systems that are used. Having a MI Addressing the so-called life-threatening issue of antibiotic resistance—which is brought on by the increase in human infections with various clinical strains of bacteria and the adoption of antibiotic resistance—requires locating reliable alternative sources. R. communis and its phytochemicals have been found to possess antibacterial properties against a range of microorganisms.(SM Al-Garni *et al.,*2018)

b. Anti fungal activity

Certain parts of R. communis, including the roots, leaves, and stems, are known to have antifungal qualities. Methanolic and aqueous extracts of R. communis have been found to be effective against a range of fungal species. An investigation into the antifungal activity of R. communis extract against several fungus species revealed that it had the highest antifungal activity against Candida albicans and the lowest activity against Alternaria solani.(SM Al-Garni *et al.,*2018)

c. Antidiabetic activity

When tested on hypoglycemic rats, the ethanolic extract of R. communis roots demonstrated promising antidiabetic effects. After alloxan diabetic rats were given a single dosage of 500 mg/kg body weight (effective dose) for 20 days, blood samples were obtained on days 0, 10, and 20 of the experiment to evaluate the lipid profile. This study significantly reduced fasting blood sugar to almost normal levels and increased insulin levels, which also improved the lipid profile and body weight. The diabetic rat's blood glucose levels decreased from 379±72 mg/dL to 149±11 mg/dL in the control group.(SM Al-Garni *et al.,*2018)

d. Anti cancer activity

In a number of studies, fractions comprising 100% ethanol, methanol, and an aqueous phase have shown promise against specific cancer cell lines, such as melanoma, MCF7 (breast cancer), HepG2 (hepatic cancer), PC3 (pancreatic cancer), and cervical cancer. Both in vitro and in vivo studies have confirmed the anti-cancer effect of R. communis using various plant components and ricin lectins.(SM Al-Garni *et al.,*2018)

e. Anti ulcer activity

It was discovered that R. communis has strong antiulcer effects. An investigation using a starting dose of 500 mg/kg has shown that R. communis possesses anti-ulcer properties. The cytoprotective action and strengthening of the stomach mucosa, which eventually leads to an improvement in mucosal defense, is the mechanism behind R. communis's anti-ulcer activity.(SM Al-Garni *et al.,*2018)

f. Analgesic activity

It was discovered that R. communis has strong central analgesic effects. Numerous investigations have been carried out to prove the analgesic properties of R. communis extract. The usual neuroleptic and central nervous system stimulant actions of R. communis extract have been investigated and demonstrated. The alkaloid ricinine in R. communis is responsible for the stimulant effects, which include clonic convulsions, memory enhancement, and hyperreactivity. Since ricinine does not inhibit the brain's exploratory behavior, it is not anxiogenic.(SM Al-Garni *et al.,*2018)

g. Hepatoprotective activity

Histopathological results also showed curative and protective propertiesof Methanolicextracts ofRicinus communis leaves against D-galactosamine intoxication.Thisobservationsuggests thatmethanolicextractof castorplant remarkablyprotected the liver from hepatitis,enhance thecurative reaction in the liver and thus can be used as a potential hepatoprotective medicine in future.The hepatoprotective activity of theRicinuscommunis is due to the membrane-stabilizing and antiperoxidative effect of flavonoids that increasethe regenerative and reparative capacity of the liver. Further,the hepatoprotective activity ofRicinus communis is protective against the necrosis of the liver along with the fatty changes.(HS Chouhan *et al.,*2021)

RICINUS COMMUNIS SEED OIL:

Castor oil is a multipurpose vegetable oil extracted from the seeds of the Ricinus communis from the family Euphorbiaceae. The castor oil contains a mixture of esters of saturated and unsaturated fatty acids such as ricinoleic, palmitic, stearic, oleic, linoleic, and linolenic acid linked to glycerol.The distinct structure of castor oil's main components provides a number of functionalization options for turning it into a cutting-edge functional material. Despite being regarded as inedible, castor oil finds extensive usage un medicine and cosmetics upon purification. Reviewing and compiling research on castor oil, its chemical makeup, various extraction techniques and their importance, and the applications of castor oil and its derivatives in industry, healthcare, and agriculture is the aim of this study. Methods: Various websites, academic research portals, and databases were used to gather the literature on castor oil and its uses. It was then sorted and presented in this review.(Satish V shirolkar *et al.,*2023)

Ricinus communis seeds are used to make castor oil, a multipurpose natural product having important nutritional and biological uses. In order to assess the physicochemical characteristics and possible uses of castor oil, this study focuses on its extraction and purification. The oil was purified to eliminate contaminants and improve its quality after being extracted using a cold-press technique to preserve its bioactive ingredients. Rich in ricinoleic acid, essential fatty acids, and antioxidants, castor oil's nutritional profile was examined to investigate its potential health benefits, such as enhancing immunity, promoting healthy skin, and facilitating digestion. Investigations were also conducted into its biomedical uses, including as a medication carrier, wound-healing agent, and bio-lubricant.This study emphasizes the value of castor oil as a sustainable substitute for synthetic components and in medicinal formulations. The difficulties of large-scale production, stable storage, and standardizing quality characteristics are also covered in the study. Prospects include investigating their potential in creating cutting-edge biomedical materials and refining extraction methods to increase production. This work adds to the growing interest in natural goods as multipurpose, environmentally friendly resources for industry and wellness.(K Takashima *et al.,*2021)

The demand for vegetable oils for industrial and residential uses has significantly expanded due to the growing global population. Vegetable oils derived from plants have been found to have a high nutritional value. The castor plant's high levels of monounsaturated fatty acids and bioactive substances make it one of the oilseeds with the highest oil content. Ricinoleic acid and other minor acids like stearic, palmitic, and oleic acid make up the majority of its fatty acid profile. Castor oil's ricinoleic acid is distinct from that of all other vegetable oils, which makes it appealing for a variety of uses. Triricinolein is the oil's main triglyceride constituent.Carotenoid, tocopherol, tocotrienol, phytosterol, phospholipid, phytochemical, and phenolic compounds are among the minor biological substances found in castor oil. These substances give the oil antioxidant, anti-inflammatory, and oxidative stability. In comparison to other vegetable oils, castor oil has good oil quality, according to the values for acid, anisidine, iodine, viscosity, and saponification. The region of production and the extraction technique used have an impact on the composition of castor oil. Ricinoleic acid and three main functional groups connected by a glycerol moiety form the core of castor oil's chemical structure.Although more research is being done on the oil's component, effective and environmentally friendly extraction techniques are still needed. The triglyceride, different fatty acids, bioactive substances, extraction techniques, and physicochemical characteristics of castor oil are thus summarized in this paper.(Kobra Shirani *et al.,*2024)

The oil's special physicochemical properties are what make it usable. In terms of chemistry, castor oil is made up of triglyceride molecules with a glycerol backbone and three esters of ricinoleic acid or ricinoleates (instead of three hydroxyl groups). Importantly, numerous studies have found that the oil contains up to 87-90% ricinoleic acid (Akpan *et al.,* 2006; Ogunniyi, 2006; Conceicao *et al.,* 2007), an 18-carbon hydroxylated monounsaturated fatty acid, with only roughly 4.2% linoleic acid, 3.0% oleic acid, 1.0% stearic and palmitic acid, 0.7% dihydroxystearic acid, and 0.3% each of linolenic and eicosanoic acids (Dave, 2002). The only commercial source of ricinoleic acid, a hydroxylated fatty acid, is castor oil. The oil is distinct from all other naturally occurring fats and oils due to its high degree of purity (by content of a single fatty acid).(EC Sandford *et al.,*2021)

HEALTH BENEFITS OF CASTOR SEED OIL:

a. In Neuorological and Msculoskeletal disorders:

Vasthi and Pana were widely used by Yogaratnakara to treat Gridhrasi, while Eranda Taila was administered with Vajeegandhadi medications are advised. For Gridhrasi, it is also suggested to take Eranda Taila along with Gomutra for a month. Eranda Taila of various origins should be consumed in Katisula with Dasamoolee Kashaya or Nagara Ambu. Patients with Amavatha, Grdhrasi, Vrddhi, etc., should take Haritaki and Eranda Taila every day in accordance with the right protocol. One lion named Eranda Taila is sufficient to appease the powerful elephant Amavatha, who roams the body (Aamavatha gajendrasya sarira vana charina, Eka eka ni hantyashu eranda Taila kesari)

b. In Gastrointestinal Disorders:

For Udara roga, Eranda Taila is suggested as Pathya.Dasamula decoction combined with Eranda Taila, taken daily, is used in Vatodara chikitsa to treat colic, dropsy, and abdominal enlargement brought on by Vata Eranda Taila should be regularly eaten with milk or cow urine for purification in Udara roga management. Eranda Taila should be taken with milk or cow urine when managing Udara roga.a lot for purification. According to the Susrtutha Samhita, licking a compound made of Eranda oil soaked in powdered Kushta and Trikatus results in hot water that works well as a purgative. Castor oil works well as a purgative when taken with a decoction of triphalas twice or three times on its own, or with milk or meat extract (Rasa). It should be recommended for young children, elderly patients, or those who are incapacitated by the symptoms of ulcers. (Rakesh Kumar Pandey *et al.,*2023)

c. In Genito Urinary Disorders:

Eranda taila added with yuvakshara and consumed relieves dysuria:in case of pain in the waist this should be consumed with decoction of dasamula or of nagara.Yavakshara and Eranda Taila were added. The patient should have oleation therapy initially, followed by purgation, and Eranda Taila mixed with milk for a month if the scrotal enlargement is caused by Vata. When combined with Gomutra, Guggulu and Eranda Taila promptly but persistently heal scrotal enlargement of Vata origin.When boiled with a decoction of Bala and properly ingested, Eranda Taila treats Antra vriddhi, or scrotal hernia, which is linked to abdominal pain and flatulence. The best way to treat Bradhna roga is to fry Abhaya paste in Eranda Taila, add Krsna and Saindhava powder, and consume it every day. (Rakesh Kumar Pandey *et al.,*2023)

d.In Vector Borne Disorders:

The Slipada (filariasis) patient who eats Gomutra and Haritaki, which are cooked in Gandharva hasta Taila (Eranda Taila), Slipada is treated every day in seven days. For Vriddhivardhma roga, it is considered Pathya. For Slipada, it is considered Pathya.It is referred to as Anala shodhana in Saligrama nighantu.Nimba and Eranda taila are Rasayanas that guard against illness. Eranda taila (Ricinus Communis Linn.) prepared with Dr. Rakesh Kumar Pandey's juice.Consuming Prasarini reduces all Dosas and is the most effective treatment for illnesses brought on by Kapha. (Rakesh Kumar Pandey *et al.,*2023)

e. In Parkinsons Disorders:

In India, R. communis leaves have long been used to treat conditions affecting the central nervous system and pain. The oil that is derived from this plant is utilized as a stimulant of motor activity in Russia. The seeds of R. communis are prescribed by Senegalese residents of Walo and Cayor to treat mental and neurological conditions. Algerians apply the oil topically to treat paralysis of the limbs. Abu Mansur treated facial paralysis with this oil in the tenth century.Known as khorve in TPM medical literature, the castor oil plant has been utilized as a treatment for a variety of illnesses.Because of its laxative qualities, it has been used in traditional medicine for more than 4,000 years. This herb has amazing effects on brain illnesses and is helpful in curing symptoms like paralysis and tremors, according to 12th-century physician Aghili Khorasani in his book Makhzan al-Adveieh. These traits are similar to those of Parkinson's disease. Castor oil (CO), which comes from R. communis, has a faint yellow color and a mild fragrance. Fatty acids make up the majority of its composition. and triglycerides, which are neutral lipids. The oil also contains a number of trace amounts of biologically active substances, including unsaponifiable fractions such phospholipids, carotenoids, phenolics, phytochemicals, phytosterols, tocopherols, and tocotrienols.(Bahareh Sadat Yousefsani *et al.,*2024)

f. In Boosting Colon Properties:

In the small intestine, castor oil, a vegetable oil extracted from the seeds of the castor oil plant, is hydrolyzed into glycerin and retinoic acid, which promotes bowel movements. The incidence of capsule excretion during battery life was 88% among patients treated with castor oil as a booster, and 70% of them had a level of bowel cleansing that was above "good." According to the tolerability questionnaire, 71% of patients expressed satisfaction with the novel colon capsule endoscopy procedure when compared to prior colonoscopies.((Kota Takashima *et al.,*2021))

g. In Eye Disorders:

Any treatment strategy is complicated by the complex pathophysiology and interactions of blepharitis, meibomian gland dysfunction, and dry eye illness. The majority of current treatments are palliative, and their effectiveness is constrained by low patient compliance and perceived inefficacy. A natural byproduct of the Ricinus communis plant, castor oil finds extensive application as an emollient in wound care products, medication delivery systems, and cosmetics. dressings. With potent antimicrobial, anti-inflammatory, anti-nociceptive, analgesic, antioxidant, wound-healing, and vaso-constrictive qualities, castor oil is considered safe and tolerated. Its primary component, ricinoleic acid, encourages the synthesis of esters, amides, and polymers due to its bipolar molecular structure. These can reduce aqueous tear evaporation and improve lipid spreading properties by supplementing physiological tear film lipids that are lacking. Research indicates that using castor oil topically to the surface of the eyes has a extended residence period, which promotes better eye surface stains, symptoms, stability, and thickness of the tear film lipid layer. The characteristics, current applications, and therapeutic potential of castor oil in the treatment of ocular surface diseases are compiled in this review.From the standpoint of ocular surface disease, the biochemical and therapeutic effects of castor oil are examined. These include oxidative and inflammatory processes, microbial and demodectic over-colonization, and clinical manifestations of pain and dryness.(EC Sandford *et al.,*2021)

HEALTH BENEFITS OF FATTY ACIDS PROFILE IN CASTOR SEED OIL:

The physical and chemical characteristics of castor oil differ depending on whether it was extracted using a solvent or by mechanical pressing. Castor oil is mostly composed of triglycerides of 12-hydroxy-9-octadecenoic acid (ricinoleic acid), which often make up more than 89% of the oil's total fatty acid content. Linoleic (4.2%), oleic (3.0%), stearic (1%), palmitic (1%), dihydroxystearic acid (0.7%), linolenic acid (0.3%), and eicosanoic acid (0.3%) are the additional fatty acid structures and percentages present in castor oil. The high concentration of ricinoleic acid, which has three functional groups, in castor oil can be used to study its chemistry.(Akwasi Yeboah *et al.,*2020)

- **Anti-inflammatory effects:** Research indicates that ricinoleic acid may help reduce inflammation, which can be beneficial in managing conditions like psoriasis.

- **Moisturizing properties:** The fatty acids in castor oil deeply penetrate and hydrate hair follicles, making it an effective moisturizer for hair and scalp health.

Known for its distinct fatty acid composition, castor seed oil (Ricinus communis) is mostly composed of ricinoleic acid, a monounsaturated fatty acid that makes up between 75 and 90 percent of the oil. While the low amounts of saturated and polyunsaturated fatty acids increase castor oil's resistance to oxidation, the high quantity of ricinoleic acid sets it apart from other vegetable oils and adds to its stability.(Akwasi Yeboah *et al.,*2020)

OIL EXTRACTION BY SOHLET METHOD AND ITS ADVANTAGES:

The Soxhlet extraction method is a widely used technique for extracting oils from solid materials. Developed by Franz Ritter von Soxhlet in 1879, it utilizes the principles of solvent reflux and siphoning to continuously extract the desired compounds.

a. Principle and Procedure:

1. **Sample Preparation:** The solid sample is finely ground to increase the surface area for extraction.
2. **Setup:** The prepared sample is placed in a thimble made of filter paper, which is then positioned inside the Soxhlet extractor. The extractor is connected to a distillation flask containing the chosen solvent and equipped with a condenser.
3. **Extraction Process:** The solvent is heated to its boiling point, causing it to evaporate and travel up into the condenser, where it cools and drips into the thimble containing the sample. The solvent dissolves the desired compounds from the sample. Once the solvent level reaches the top of the siphon tube, it siphons back into the distillation flask, carrying the extracted compounds with it. This cycle repeats multiple times, allowing for efficient extraction. (Ghulam Hussain *et al.,* 2023)

b. Applications:

Soxhlet extraction is commonly employed in various fields:

- **Oil Extraction:** It's used to extract oils from seeds and other plant materials. For instance, studies have utilized Soxhlet extraction to obtain oil from rapeseed and ka
- **Essential Oils:** The method has been applied to extract essential oils from plant materials, such as anise seeds. (Ghulam Hussain *et al.,* 2023)
- **Biofuel Research:** Researchers have used Soxhlet extraction to extract oils from algae for potential biodiesel production.

c. Advantages:

- **Efficiency:** The continuous extraction process ensures thorough extraction of the desired compounds.
- **Solvent Economy:** The same solvent is recycled through the system, reducing the amount needed.(Sukasri *et al.,* 2023)

d. Considerations:

- **Thermal Degradation:** The high temperatures involved may lead to the degradation of heat-sensitive compounds.
- **Extraction Time:** The process can be time-consuming, depending on the sample and solvent used.

In Soxhlet extraction is a valuable technique for extracting oils and other compounds from solid materials, offering efficiency and solvent economy, though considerations regarding thermal degradation and extraction time should be taken into account.

CONCLUSION

Castor (Ricinus communis) seeds possess significant functional properties that have attracted growing interest in the fields of medicine, agriculture, and industry. Rich in bioactive compounds such as ricinoleic acid, flavonoids, alkaloids, and phenolic compounds, castor seeds exhibit diverse pharmacological activities including antimicrobial, antioxidant, anti-inflammatory, and analgesic effects. The unique composition of castor oil, primarily consisting of ricinoleic acid, contributes to its application in pharmaceuticals, cosmetics, and bio-lubricants. Additionally, castor seed extracts show potential in wound healing, skin care formulations, and traditional medicine for treating various ailments. Despite its beneficial properties, the presence of toxic compounds like ricin necessitates careful processing and detoxification to ensure safety for therapeutic use. The agricultural utility of castor plants, particularly their ability to grow in marginal soils with minimal inputs, highlights their potential in sustainable crop production systems. Furthermore, castor seeds are emerging as a renewable resource for the production of biodiesel and biodegradable plastics, contributing to environmental sustainability. In conclusion, castor seeds offer multifaceted functional properties with promising applications in health care, industry, and environmental conservation. Future research focused on safe extraction methods and value-added product development will further enhance the commercial and therapeutic potential of Ricinus communis seeds.

REFERENCE

1. Akwasi, Y., Sheng, Y., Jiannong, L., Yu, X., Hanna, A. D., Kwadwo Gyapong Agyenim, B., Miao, C., & Xuegui, Y. (2021). Castor oil (Ricinus communis): A review on the chemical composition and physicochemical properties. *Food Science and Technology*, 41(suppl 2), 399–413
2. Akande, T. O., Odunsi, A. A., Olabode, O. S., & Ojediran, T. K. (2012). Physical and nutrient characterisation of raw and processed castor (Ricinus communis L.) seeds in Nigeria. *World Journal of Agricultural Sciences*, 8(1), 89–95.
3. Vasco-Leal, J. F., Mosquera-Artamonov, J. D., Hernández-Ríos, I., Méndez-Gallegos, S. J., Perea-Flores, M. J., Peña-Aguilar, J. M., & Rodríguez-García, M. E. (2018). Physicochemical characteristics of seeds from wild and cultivated castor bean plants (Ricinus communis L.). *Ingeniería e Investigación*, 38(1), 24–30.
4. Raharjo, T. J., Utami, W., Fajr, A., & Haryadi, W. (2021). Antibacterial peptides from tryptic hydrolysate of Ricinus communis seed protein fractionated using cation exchange chromatography. *International Journal of Peptide Research and Therapeutics*, 27(1), 123–132.
5. Galal, T. M., Essa, B., & Al-Yasi, H. M. (2021). Heavy metals uptake and its impact on the growth dynamics of the riparian shrub Ricinus communis L. along Egyptian heterogenic habitats. *Environmental Science and Pollution*

Research, 28(10), 12345–12358
6. Mutlu, H., & Meier, M. A. R. (2010). Castor oil as a renewable resource for the chemical industry. *European Journal of Lipid Science and Technology*, 112(1), 10–30.
7. Scarpa, A., & Guerci, A. (1982). Various uses of the castor oil plant (Ricinus communis L.): A review. *Journal of Ethnopharmacology*, 5(2), 117–137
8. Ogunniyi, D. S. (2006). Castor oil: A vital industrial raw material. *Bioresource Technology*, 97(9), 1086–1091.
9. Barnes, D., Baldwin, B. S., & Braasch, D. A. (2009). Degradation of ricin in castor seed meal by temperature and chemical treatment. *Industrial Crops and Products*, 29(2–3), 509–515
10. Atanasov, A. G., Waltenberger, B., Pferschy-Wenzig, E. M., Linder, T., Wawrosch, C., Uhrin, P & Stuppner, H. (2015). Discovery and resupply of pharmacologically active plant-derived natural products: A review. *Biotechnology Advances*, 33(8), 1582–1614

CHAPTER 7

GREEN FOOD PACKAGING FROM AGRO WASTE

Murali Krishna K

Department of Food Science and Nutrition, Nehru Arts and Science College, Coimbatore, Tamil Nadu-641 105

INTRODUCTION

Food packaging plays a vital role in preserving the safety, quality, and shelf life of food products. It helps protect food from contamination and extends its usability during transportation and storage. However, the growing reliance on food packaging, particularly plastic, has become a significant source of environmental pollution. Packaging contributes not only to waste but also to various environmental concerns, including landfills, oceanic pollution, and resource depletion. While food packaging helps reduce food waste, it also raises environmental concerns, particularly as packaging waste continues to grow due to high consumption in the food sector. (Kenneth Marsh, Ph.D *et al.,*2007)

Advances in food processing and food packaging play a primary role in keeping the U.S. food supply among the safest in the world. Simply stated, packaging maintains the benefits of food processing after the process is complete, enabling foods to travel safely for long distances from their point of origin and still be wholesome at the time of consumption. However, packaging technology must balance food protection with other issues, including energy and material costs, heightened social and environmental consciousness, and strict regulations on pollutants and disposal of municipal solid waste. Municipal solid waste (MSW) consists of items commonly thrown away, including packages, food scraps, yard trimmings, and durable items such as refrigerators and computers. Legislative and regulatory efforts to control packaging are based on the mistaken perception that packaging is the major burden of MSW. Instead, the U.S. Environmental Protection Agency (EPA) found that approximately only 31% of the MSW generated in 2005 was from packaging-related materials, including glass, metal, plastic, paper, and paperboard—a percentage that has remained relatively constant since the 1990s despite an increase in the total amount of MSW. (Fehlberg *et al.,* 2020; (Rathinavel & Saravanakumar, 2021)

Non Packaging sources such as newsprint, telephone books, and office communication generate more than twice as much MSW (EPA 2006a). Food is the only product class typically consumed 3 times per day by every person. Consequently, food packaging accounts for almost two-thirds of total packaging waste by volume (Hunt and others 1990). Moreover, food packaging is approximately 50% (by weight) of total packaging sales. Although the specific knowledge available has changed since publication of the 1st Scientific Status Summary on the relationship between packaging and MSW (IFT 1991), the issue remains poorly understood, complicating efforts to address the environmental impact of discarded packaging materials. This article describes the role of food packaging in the food supply chain, the types of materials used in food packaging, and the impact of food packaging on the environment. In addition, this document provides an overview of EPA's solid waste management guidelines and other waste management options. Finally, it addresses disposal methods and legislation on packaging disposal (KENNETH MARSH, PH.D 2022)

The principal roles of food packaging are to protect food products from outside influences and damage, to contain the food, and to provide consumers with ingredient and nutritional information (Coles 2003). Traceability, convenience, and tamper indication are secondary functions of increasing importance. The goal of food packaging is to contain food in a costeffective way that satisfies industry requirements and consumer desires, maintains food safety, and minimizes environmental impact. (BETTY BUGUSU, PH.D 2019)

HISTORY

For millennia, humans stored their food in containers they found in nature—dried gourds, shells, hollow logs, leaves—as well as baskets and pottery. By the first century BC, the Chinese were wrapping foods with treated tree bark and other forerunners of paper. Centuries later, Napoleon Bonaparte used some of the first mass-produced canned food to feed his troops in the FrancoAustrian War of 1809. Plastics were discovered in the decades following that innovation but not used beyond military purposes until well into the twentieth century.1,2 The art and science of food packaging have evolved a long way from those origins. Today, products often are wrapped in multiple layers of packaging to get them safely from the point of manufacture to consumers' cupboards and refrigerators. Food packaging can improve food safety by alleviating bacterial contamination. It has been proposed that increased use of packaging for fresh produce could prevent contamination with Salmonella spp., a leading cause of foodborne diseases.3"We appreciate foodservice packaging because of the convenience it affords for our busy lifestyles, but often we forget about the main benefit: sanitation," says Lynn Dyer, president of the Foodservice Packaging Institute, an industry association. "That's why single-use products were invented over100 years ago—to help stop the spread of contagious diseases." In addition to preventing bacterial contamination, food packaging also extend the shelf life of products, which allows for broader distribution and reduced food waste. Food waste is a significant problem in the United States. The Environmental Protection Agency (EPA) estimates that34 million tons of food was thrown away in 2010, representing close to 14% of the municipal solid waste generated in the United States.4 (Ironically, using more packaging to reduce food waste creates another waste problem: In 2010 household packaging constituted almost one-third of the municipal solid waste generated.5)In the United States, all food-contact substances (FCSs)— defined as substances "intended for use as a component of materials used in manufacturing, packing, pack-aging, transporting, or holding food if such use is not intended to have any technical effect in such food"6 —are regulated by the Food and Drug Administration (FDA).Different packaging materials offer different advantages. Glass preserves taste well and is chemically inert. Paper and paperboard are economic to produce and easy to print on. They are also lightweight, which reduces the fuel used for the transport of goods.7Steel and aluminum offer the advantages of malleability, impermeability, and ease of recycling. Aluminum can also be bound to paper or plastic films for more versatility in the types of packaging that can be produced. And plastics have revolutionized the packaging industry because they are highly moldable into infinite shapes, lightweight, inexpensive, easy to seal, and durable. (l Chen 2021)

Migration in foods

It is well known that chemical components from packaging can migrate into foods, but questions of how much migration occurs and what the potential health effects may bear e gaining more attention from researcher sand regulators.8 However, few studies to date have looked at adverse human health effects of these exposures. Different types of packaging material spose different potential chemical exposures. Glass, for instance, is generally recognized as safe by the FDA when used as a container for holding food. But some glass bottles and Jars may contain lead. Researchers at the Institute of Environmental Geochemistry of the University of Heidelberg in Germany assessed 125 brands of drinking water from28 countries and showed that waters packaged in glass bottles contained 26–57 times more lead than comparable waters bottled in polyethylene terephthalate (PET) plastic. The increased lead content appeared to be a result of leaching from glass containers, although at < 1–761 ng/L, even the highest lead levels detected were well below maximum allowances for drinking water (10 µg/L in the European Union and Canada, and 15 µg/L in the United States).9Other studies have found chemical contamination of food coming not from glass itself but from materials used to seal the metal lids on glass jars. In work by a Danish group, some foods in glass jars sealed with polyvinyl chloride (PVC) gaskets were found to contain di(2-ethylhexyl)phthalate(DEHP) and other phthalates at levels deemed unacceptable by the European Food Safety Authority.10,11 These studies did not assess potential health effects from this exposure, but in other studies phthalate shave been associated with endocrine disruption in humans.12,13,14Environmental health concerns associated with the use of paper food packaging have focused on the use of recycled paper products. Printing inks from earlier in carnations of the paper can be trapped in this material potentially exposing consumers to phthalates as well as to other suspected endocrine disruptors, including mineral oils.(AM dakhel , A Adnan 2019)

A study conducted by a German group showed that infant foods packed in recycled paperboard boxes with coated paper liners were contaminated with di isobutyl phthalate and di-n-butyl phthalate, with a few samples containing the former at levels exceeding European Commission limits for food contaminants.15 The authors noted that inner liners made of aluminum-coated foil were much more effective than coated paper at blocking the migration of phthalates from recycled paperboard packaging. There also have been problems with the liners themselves in some paper boxes. In2010 Kellogg Company recalled 28 million boxes of cereal because of elevated levels ofmethylnaphthalene16 that leached from the coated paper lining the boxes.(l Chen 2021)

Although the potential consequences of ingestion of this compound are not well understood,atleast five consumers reportedly became ill after eating the contaminated cereal.Perhaps the hottest current debate regarding food packaging is the use of epoxy-based resins containing bi phenol A (BPA) in metal can liners (BPA is also used in hard, clear polycarbonate plastic).19 In 2008 the National Toxicology Program released a review of the evidence on the toxicity of BPA expressing" some concern" that the compound may adversely affect the brain and prostate gland in fetuses, infants, and children at exposure levels documented in the general U.S. population. The Natural Resources Defense Council has petitioned the FDA to ban the use of BPA in food packaging, but on30 March 2012 the FDA issued an interim ruling denying that request, pending furtherresearch.21 Currently the FDA allows the use of BPA in food-contact applications (BETTY BUGUSU, PH.D 2019)

Food Safety (10 µg/kg/day) and the U.S.EPA (50 µg/kg/day). Despite the relatively low estimated doses from eating any one food, these authors and others 8,23 point out there are multiple sources of intake of BPA ,and evidence increasingly suggests that BPA and other endocrine disruptors—like the hormones they mimic—may cause unexpected effects even at tiny doses, although he extent to which these effects may occur in humans is still under investigation.24Some chemicals of concern, such asphthalates , have been phased out of use in food packaging. For instance, the American Plastics Council has stated that "a phthalates are not used in plastic beverage bottles, no rare they used in plastic food wrap, food containers, or any other type of plastic food packaging sold in the United States."25 Steve Russell, vice president of the Plastics Division of the American Chemistry Council, says that in the United States very little PVC is used in food contact except for meat and cling wrap, and in that application, phthalates have been replaced with alternative plasticizers such as di-(2-ethylhexyl) adipate .Adipates have been shown to potentially leach into foods, and their effects are being studied in laboratory animals, but effects on humans if any—are not known. (Luz Claudio}

Plastics have remained the material of choice, and after serving their intended purpose, a large proportion ends up in the environment where they persist for centuries. The packaging industry is the largest and growing consumer of synthetic plastics derived from fossil fuels. Food packaging plastics account for the bulk of plastic waste that are polluting the environment. Additionally, given the fact that petroleum reserves are finite and facing depletion, there is a need for the development of alternative materials that can serve the same purpose as conventional plastics. This paper reviews the function of packaging materials and highlights the future potential of the adoption of green materials. Biopolymers have emerged as promising green materials although they still have very low market uptake. Polylactic acid (PLA) has emerged as the most favoured bioplastic. However, it is limited by its high cost and some performance drawbacks. Blending with agricultural waste and natural fillers can result in green composites at low cost, low greenhouse gas emissions, and with improved performance for food packaging applications. The continent of Africa is proposed as a rich source of fibres and fillers that can be sustainably exploited to fabricate green composites in a bid to achieve a circular economy . (albert uchennaude)

usage of non-biodegradable materials for the various packaging applications has raised environmental pollution concerns [1,2]. Food packaging accounts for the biggest growing sector within the synthetic plastic packaging market domain [3,4,5,6,7]. Large amounts of different materials, like paper, glass and plastics, are used globally to manufacture packaging materials and more than two thirds are used in the food sector alone. This amount is growing unceasingly as a result of changes occurring in habits of food preparation and consumption, as well as the positive development of various areas and markets in the world . The packaging industry consumes the highest volumes of plastics produced globally and is the main source supplying waste plastics into the environment at an alarming rate . This can be attributed to single-use plastics and the increase of on- the-go snacks and ready-made meals that imply the once-off use of durable plastic packaging material. As a result, there is increasing need for eco-friendly sustainable packaging materials with the desired physical, mechanical and barrier properties for food packaging.(Khalil, H.A.; Davoudpour, Y.; Saurabh, C.K.;

Environmental impact is a prime consideration in food packaging and in the food packaging industry. Perhaps the most adverse effect upon the environment as perceived by the public is the visual effect of packaging litter, but on careful reflection the environmental impact can be seen in several ways (20): (a) litter, (b) usage of raw materials for packaging purposes, (c) ease and convenience of packaging disposal, (d) adverse consequences of careless disposal of packaging, (e) feasibility of recycling or reuse, and (f) energy content, comprising the energy equivalents of the materials themselves, the energy consumed in their manufacture and use, and the energy implications of conversion and packaging operations,transport, collection after use, and disposal. It is obvious that there is no single solution to the problem of the environmental impact of food packaging. Rather, a set of approaches should be used, each of which has a distinctive role to play. Future packaging operations should certainly seek to minimize environmental impact, based upon choosing the most advantageous postuse options and upon a quantitative life-cycle analysis of the package. However, there should be taken into consideration the complete system of food disposal from the producer to the consumer to bring about an overall environmental benefit, not only by reducing the environmental impact of the packaging material itself but also by reducing food waste and improving distribution and storage times.(JS Yaradoddi 2022)

In future, designers and manufacturers of packaging will be expected to play a major role in the conservation of the environment and the prevention of wastes and to collaborate with public authorities to set up systems guaranteeing reduction, reusing, and recycling aspects, and forcing research to identify new environmental- friendly, and even edible, packaging materials. Nowadays, on this issue, interest seems to have shifted from biodegradability to recycling, since so many products from recycled material are now available, and recycling may be regarded as one of the most important reasons for preferring a particular package type. Environmental impact is a prime consideration in food packaging and in the food packaging industry. Perhaps the most adverse effect upon the environment as perceived by the public is the visual effect of packaging litter, but on careful reflection the environmental impact can be seen in several ways (20): (a) litter, (b) usage of raw materials for packaging purposes, (c) ease and convenience of packaging disposal, (d) adverse consequences of careless disposal of packaging, (e) feasibility of recycling or reuse, and (f) energy content, comprising the energy equivalents of the materials themselves, the energy consumed in their manufacture and use, and the energy implications of conversion and packaging operations, transport, collection after use, and disposal. It is obvious that there is no single solution to the problem of the environmental impact of food packaging. Rather, a set of approaches should be used, each of which has a distinctive role to play. Future packaging operations should certainly seek to minimize environmental impact, based upon choosing the most advantageous postuse options and upon a quantitative life-cycle analysis of the package.

However, there should be taken into consideration the complete system of food disposal from the producer to the consumer to bring about an overall environmental benefit, not only by reducing the environmental impact of the packaging material itself but also by reducing food waste and improving distribution and storage times. In future, designers and manufacturers of packaging will be expected to play a major role in the conservation of the environment and the prevention of wastes and to collaborate with public authorities to set up systems guaranteeing reduction, reusing, and recycling aspects, and forcing research to identify new environmental- friendly, and even edible, packaging materials. Nowa- days, on this issue, interest seems to have shifted from biodegradability to recycling, since so many products from recycled material are now available, and recycling may be regarded as one of the most important reasons for preferring a particular package type. 1 LITCHFIELD, J.H.

Some wastes and effluents with environmental impact derived from the agricultural and food processing industry are inevitable. Their composition is extremely varied depending on both the nature of the product and the production techniques employed, resulting in vari- ous pollution effects of the different food processing industries. There are, however, certain characteristics of particular food processing industries as described above which may be useful in evaluating pollution factors and, as a consequence, in applying appropriate treatment operations for environmental protection objectives. Generally, attention must be placed on minimization of waste through advanced manufacturing practices, and constructive utilization of what is unvoidable by recycling and bioprocessing of by- products and waste into edible food, feed, [Type text] fuel, and chemicals with industrial application in order to pre- vent pollution and minimize the effects of effluents on the environment. Research work is urgently needed that will help the entire agricultural and food process- ing industry identify, develop, and implement new and better systems for producing high-quality and economical foods with reduced adverse effects on the environ- ment and better utilization of the raw materials. In our time of environmental concern, much greater efforts are required to solve the problems of air emissions, water discharges, and too much waste. Appropriate technologies, techniques, processes, and treatment methods are available to a great extent for the different types of the food processing industry.

Nevertheless, further environmental-related research is needed to evaluate:

(a) the qualitative and quantitative chemical composition of the solid, liquid, and gaseous by- products and wastes, as well as the extent to which they are released to the environment, (b) the environmental media into which they are discharged, (c) the qual- itative and quantitative environmental impact of wastes and by-products from the food processing industry, (d) the available techniques for waste recovery and re- utilization, and effective methods for waste bioconversion and upgrading in order to minimize environmental pollution, (e) improved packaging technologies to reduce the quantity of solid waste and environmental impact thereof, (f) alternatives to toxic chemicals used in agricultural and food processing operations, and (g) policy and authority options which should be aimed at controlling and strengthening existing environmental regulations, or even posing stricter requirements. Last but not least, increased efforts should be concentrated in the motivation of the consumers, producers, and authorities to conserve energy, water and raw materials, and to minimize the generation of waste materials by re- utilization and upgrading techniques, and, in consequence, to prevent pollution of the environment. In conclusion, it can be presumed that by a systematic approach to all the environmental problems associated with the agricultural and food processing industry, these can be reduced to very low levels both economically and technically, providing

BIODEGRADABLE PACKAGING MATRERIAL – SCPOE AND IMPORTANCE

Agro-waste is a rich source of bio compounds with high potential as a raw material for food packaging. Utilization of agro-waste supports the goal of sustainable development in a circular economy. Harvested agro-produce must be properly handled, processed, packed, and stored, especially during transportation. Appropriate protocols should be followed to prevent food loss and waste throughout the supply chain . Packaging, especially conventional plastic packaging, is a large source of waste and environmental pollution. Appropriate packaging should serve four main functions for food applications, namely protection, containment, convenience, and communication, which are essential to ensure quality and safety in food consumption. A wide variety of materials is used as packaging. Recent developments in packaging technology include the evolution of active and smart packaging, where active antioxidant, antimicrobial, flavoring, and oxygen-scavenging agents are added to supplement the desired packaging characteristics and enhance shelf life. However, increasing concerns have been expressed about the use of fossil-based plastic packages for food coverings, which negatively impact the environment. Therefore, alternative eco-friendly packaging materials are now preferred by both global consumers and the packaging industry (Sandhya Alice Varghese 2023)

Eco-friendly packages can serve the purpose of sustainable food protection. Food packaging is mainly utilized as a single-usage wrap and this triggers the waste generated by the plastic packaging industry. Bio plastics are sustainable materials for the packaging industry. However, these environmentally friendly plastics have certain drawbacks. The biodegradability of bio plastics is affected by temperature and most end up in landfill mixed with other recyclable plastics, Therefore, packaging made from bio resources requires the input of modern technology to improve the required properties (Sonchaeng, U 2022)

The increased environmental concern of global consumers has driven the research and development of alternative packaging materials. Numerous biomaterials derived from bio resources have shown potential for use as packaging. Agro-waste is a rich source of biopolymers and bioactive compounds. Extraction and purification of these materials as alternative packaging boosts sustainable development. Agro-waste as it is generally known, is the leftovers derived from the generation and processing of various agro-products, including fruits, vegetables, meat, and dairy products. Rapid urbanization and population growth as well as industrial growth have generated vast quantities of solid waste that have now become a major social problem. Annual generation of agro-waste has mushroomed, and without proper disposal methods this causes environmental pollution as well as health hazards for both humans and animals. Most agroindustrial wastes are rich in bio-compounds that are poorly treated and underutilized. Over one billion tons of solid waste are generated annually, polluting the environment and producing socioeconomic ill effects. This is a wake-up call for the proper management of an enormous amount of waste. Researchers are actively seeking new, innovative, and eco-friendly technologies for waste management. With its huge availability and potential economic value, agro-waste utilization is now considered an important aspect of sustainability. (Hussain ,C;Singh, S.2021)

Affecting the recycling system structure. Bio plastics are also relatively costly, which limits their application, and they have limited mechanical and barrier properties.The waste that could be utilized in the packaging material field must be categorized as nonhazardous solid waste for further safe usage. Waste management, including recycling and utilization, has been regulated by the Resource Conservation and Recovery Act (RCRA) under the Environmental Protection Agency (EPA, US); they have specified the recycled materials that must be excluded from solid waste in processing; (i) waste used as an ingredient; (ii) waste used as a product substitute; and (iii) waste returned to the production process. Waste can be used as an ingredient if the waste was directly included in the ingredient in the production process. Waste can be used as a product substitute when the material is directly used to replace an [Type text] existing product without first being reclaimed, while wastes can be returned to the production process when the material is returned to the production process as a feedstock or as raw material. Agricultural waste is one of the excluded hazardous wastes and is defined as a solid waste generated by the growing and harvesting of agricultural crops or the raising of animals, including animal manures, which are returned to the soil as fertilizers.(Resource Conservation and Recovery Act (RCRA)2022)

Agro-waste has recently been intensively studied, generating a wide range of valuable materials including biofuels, enzymes, vitamins, antioxidants, animal feed, antibiotics, and other chemicals. Materials derived from agro-waste such as cellulose, hemicellulose, chitin, lignin, starch, pectin, alginate, and protein have the potential to be turned into food packaging, with several advantages such as non- toxicity, biodegradability, wide availability, and biocompatibility with other materials, which can improve the quality of the packaged materials and extend shelf life (Oyeoka, H.C.; Ewulonu, C.M 2021)

Fruit peel contains components which are extracted and utilized in different products. One of the components is pectin. Among other fruits citrus peel is one of the most important sources of commercial pectin. Pectin is a natural, biocompatible, biodegradable, and reusable polysaccharide classified as an emulsifier, gelling agent, glazing agent, stabilizer, and/or thickener in commercial applications of food processing industries. The utilization of fruit peels as edible coating material can also be the promising aspect of food packaging industries. Pectin based coatings and the food products developed from the by-product of fruits, i.e., peel, are an important material innovation and sustainable food waste management approach because it not only reduces the amount of by-products obtained from the food processing industries but it also decreases dependence on petroleum while still yielding a product that provides similar benefits of traditional plastics where the quality of fruits and vegetable's shelf life are increased.(Girish N. Mathad 2021)

Edible coatings are made up of thin layers applied on the surface of the food to make its shelf life longer, maintain the properties, characteristics and functionality of foods at minimum cost . This application can increase its functionality by extending the shelf life, preventing the microbial spoilage and acting as a carrier matrix for antimicrobial agents (Raghav, P.K.; Agarwal, 2016).

Coating can be considered as an effective method of preservation during transport of fruits and vegetables easily affected by microorganisms, insects, pre- and postharvesting conditions. Coatings also help in developing a modified atmosphere to induce varied alterations in minimally processed and fresh foodstuff in various areas such as sensory quality, antioxidant properties, color, firmness, ethylene production, microbial growth inhibition and organic compounds under anaerobic processes . Recently, essential oils (EOs) and their main components have received substantial attention due to the presence of effective antimicrobial properties in them. The EOs are commonly considered as safe, as they impart maximum effects with the minimum change in the organoleptic properties of the food (Alparslan, Y et al.2017)

In the development of edible coatings applications of this emerging technology included a variety of nanosystems, consisting of nanoemulsions, polymeric nanoparticles and nanocomposites to release antioxidants, and showing antibacterial activities on the surface of the food. Because of the many phenolic substances with excellent antioxidant capacity, fruits and vegetable peel are considered as suitable materials for inclusion into films and coatings. Fish gelatin is believed to be a valuable biopolymer source for fabricating biofilms because of its biodegradable nature and high myofibrillar protein content . Additionally, because of the variations in the sequence of amino acid, fruit and vegetable peel-based films show less water permeability in contrast to mammalian gelatin-based film (Guerrero, P et al 2017)

Advantages of Agro-Waste Films are Sustainability, biodegradability, low cost and customization. Agro-waste is a renewable resource, and using it to produce biodegradable films helps to reduce the environmental impact of plastic waste. Unlike conventional plastics, agrowaste films break down naturally over time, reducing long-term environmental pollution. Since agro-waste is often an underutilized by-product of agricultural processes, it can be an inexpensive raw material

Customize the properties of these biodegradable films can be modified by adjusting the blend of agro-waste, biopolymers, and additives, allowing for a wide range of applications. Mechanical Properties: Agro-waste films may have weaker mechanical properties compared to synthetic plastics, such as lower tensile strength or reduced durability. Moisture Sensitivity Many agro-based films are more sensitive to moisture and may lose structural integrity when exposed to high humidity or water. Processing Difficulties: Extracting usable polymers from agro- waste can be complex, requiring specialized equipment and chemical treatments, which can increase production costs. using agro-waste for the production of biodegradable films has the potential to revolutionize packaging and reduce plastic pollution. By harnessing the abundant supply of agricultural byproducts, researchers can create sustainable alternatives to conventional plastics that are both environmentally friendly and economically feasible.(Rehan *et al.,* 2018).

GROUNDNUT SHELL POWDER AND ORANGE PEEL POWDER AVAILABILITY AND USAGE GROUNDNUT SHELL POWDER

The groundnut is regarded as the third most important oilseed crop worldwide. Groundnut is a popular oilseed crop that can be grown, especially in tropical areas. The groundnut (Arachis hypogeae) is a member of the Leguminoseae family and is also known as earthnuts, pygmy nuts, and pig nuts, peanuts and monkey nuts are frequently consumed by locals. India is the fourth largest producer of oilseeds in the world, next to the United States, China, and Brazil. It produces approximately 32.10 metric tons of oilseeds annually, or 2.7% of the world's oilseed production. The crops are grown on an area of nearly 26 million ha, or 19% of the world's oil seeds area, and their annual average yield is 1224 kg/ha (Anon 2017).

A variety of oilseeds, including groundnut, rapeseed, and mustard, soybean,sesame, sunflower linseed, Niger seed, castor, and two perennial oilseeds (coconut and palm oil), can thrive in India's diverse agro-ecological environments. Groundnut production worldwide hit a record high of approximately 46.01 MT (Anon 2020).

In terms of groundnut production, India, China, the United States, West Africa, Sudan, and Nigeria are the most significant nations. According to Anon 2020, India has the most land area in the world— 8.5 million hectares, or 14% of the world's production. Protein is abundant in groundnuts. It has between 47% and 49% oil and 20% protein. The fiber contains 18.7% hemicellulose, 35.7% cellulose, 30.2% lignin, and 5.9% ash . There are numerous varieties of Indian groundnuts available; Red Natal, Java, Spanish Bold, or Runner. It is available throughout the year and is mostly grown in a rain-fed environment in India. The states of Uttar Pradesh, Madhya Pradesh, Rajasthan, Gujarat, Maharashtra, Karnataka, Andhra Pradesh, and Tamil Nadu contribute the most to groundnut cultivation. In Punjab all out region under groundnut crop is 1000 hectare each year and all out creation of groundnut is 3000 metric tons (Kaur P 2019).

After removing the groundnut seed from its pod, the product that remains is known as groundnut shells. Under natural conditions, this is the prevalent agro-industrial waste product with a very slow rate of degradation. Groundnut shells contain cellulose, hemicelluloses and lignin miniature fibrils, which are assembled into full scale fibrils. According to Zheng et al (2013),Peanut shell fiber contains cellulose (35.5%), hemicelluloses (18.7%), lignin (30.2%), and ash (5.9%). It is utilized as a feedstock, food, filler in fertilizer, and even as a carrier for bio filters in the commercial sector. However, the majority of abandoned groundnut shells are either burned or buried, which pollutes the environment. Therefore, new technologies must be developed to achieve zero waste production and put this otherwise useless product to use in the food, feed, paper, and bioenergy industries (Sheelendra and Shilpa, 2014; Bishnu et al (2018)

Because rotten waste biomass emits methane, leachate, and other harmful compounds, the sudden increase in both quantity and type of agricultural waste is making its management and utilization a difficult challenge. Due to the greenhouse effect, farmers burning crop residues in open fields release a significant amount of carbon dioxide gas and other pollutants. The utilization of plastic and its related applications is non biodegradable , and further more goes through non sustainable oil based commodities. Most biodegradable polymers are made from waste from the processing industry, marine food, and agricultural feedstock. Currently, research is gradually being directed toward the creation of a biodegradable food packaging system to lessen environmental impact. Because of their low cost, biocompatibility, non-toxicity, biodegradability, and ready availability, naturally occurring biodegradable materials have gained a lot of popularity in recent years for the production of biopolymers. As a source of raw materials, agricultural feed stock and byproducts have emerged as a viable alternative to conventional woody materials that is renewable and long-lasting. According to Andjelkovic et al (2005)

Different kinds of petroleum-based packaging materials are used for food packaging, which pollutes the environment. Therefore, biodegradable and polymer-based films need to be developed in order to reduce the drawbacks of synthetic petroleum-based packaging systems and ensure that packed materials remain stable for a predetermined amount of time. Biopolymers are mostly needed in the food packaging industry to slow the rate and spread of environmental problems. Biopolymers are materials derived from plants, animal products, and microbial products. The most widely available polymer with strength and stiffness is cellulose. Hemicelluloses, waxed resins, lignin, and other substances include cellulose. Cellulose is made from plant materials like wood, cotton, sisal, coconut fiber, and microscopic organisms like tunicates and others, as well as materials that don't come from plants. Its structure resembles a lignin network of fibrils. In light of its biodegradability, bioavailability and thermodependability, it very well may be utilized as an option in contrast to oil and manufactured based items. The cellulose-based food packaging film would be transparent, strong, flexible, and clear. Due to its hydrophilic and excellent mechanical properties, this cellulose's use in food product packaging has increased. Tasdemir *et al.,* 2019) Plastic is the most common packaging material. it being non degradable material, is creating environmental hazards. It has been rightly banned by the government. A world wide search is on for developing suitable biodegradable alternatives for packaging fruits, vegetables, flowers, milk, meat, frozen foods, ready-t-eat foods, etc. therefore the study is very relevant to the present day. Groundnut shells are the most common conventional materials that are being tested as a replacement for plastic filler in all kinds of plastic products and packaging. Because of these properties, groundnut shells are used as the material for packaging. Groundnut shell powder, which is made from agricultural waste and is biodegradable, can be used to make bionanocomposite film, which could be used by high-end businesses.(Molina-Calle *et al.,* 2015)

Cellulose, hemicellulose, lignin, protein, and ash are all components of the chemical structure of Groun shells . The primary structural element of plant cell walls is cellulose. Cellulose is a glucose molecule with beta (1–4) linked chain . Hemicellulose, a complex carbohydrate, gives plant cell walls strength and stability. Plant cell walls are them stiffness and strength. Ash is an inorganic substance that is still present after organic material has been burned. Protein is an energy-rich organic molecule that provides a source of fuel for the plant.

POTENTIAL APPLICATION

Peanut-shell-powder composites have garnered significant attention in various industrial sectors due to their unique properties and sustainable nature. In the automotive industry, these composites find applications in interior components such as door panels, dashboard trims, and seat structures. They offer excellent mechanical properties, including high strength, impact resistance, and dimensional stability, making them suitable for lightweight and eco-friendly automotive parts. Furthermore, their natural fibers provide aesthetic appeal and can contribute to reducing the overall weight of vehicles, improving fuel efficiency. Shahi, N.2021

In the packaging industry, peanut-shell-powder composites are utilized for the production of food packaging films. These composites offer desirable barrier properties, such as resistance to moisture, gases, and UV radiation, making them suitable for food packaging applications. Additionally, their biodegradability and renewable nature make them an environmentally friendly alternative to conventional packaging materials. A recent study by Usman et al

The peanut shell and skin powder was used to prepare the film-forming solution. The film-forming solution was mixed with starch and chitosan and prepared a film. With the addition of peanut shell and skin extracts, the viscosity of the starch–chitosan filmforming solution was reduced. The water vapor permeability and swelling of the film was decreased with the addition of peanut shell and peanut skin extracts. The hydrophilicity of the film was greatly influenced by peanut shell extracts compared to peanut skin extracts. The color and opacity of the film were both improved by both extracts. And the starch–chitosan film infused with peanut skin extracts had greater antioxidant power than the composite film infused with peanut shell extracts. The tensile strength of the film was decreased by the addition of peanut shell extract and the tensile strength of the film was improved with the addition of peanut skin extract. In order to create bio-nano composite food-packaging film, Raj et al

Three types of films were prepared by using agar solution (AS), peanut shell powder (PSP), and cellulose microfiber (CMF) synthesized from peanut shell powder. When compared to the other two films, the CMF film exhibited good mechanical characteristics. The tensile strength and Young's modulus of CMF film were found to be 49.4 ± 4.3 and 1.71 ± 0.07, respectively, which were greater than the values for AS film and PSP film. The CMF films exhibited improvement in water solubility and opacity compared with the other two films. Due to their advantageous benefits, CMF films can be used as a substitute for petroleum products, as a natural filler, and as a way to turn agricultural waste into a useful product. They can also be utilized in a variety of applications, including food packaging and tissue engineering, among others. Jayaraj et al. prepared a green composite film for food packaging application by using nano cellulose synthesized from peanut shell. The composite film was prepared using chitosan, iron nanoparticles, and nano cellulose. The biodegradable polymer-based film prepared from CNCs showed high degradation temperature, which demonstrated high thermal stability. Due to this, these films can be successfully used as packaging material to extend the shelf life of food products. Jayaraj, K.; Christy, J.S.2020

The construction sector benefits from peanut-shell-powder composites in various applications. These composites can be used for manufacturing decking materials, flooring, ceiling tiles, and insulation panels. They possess excellent thermal insulation properties, fire resistance, and durability, contributing to energy- efficient and sustainable building solutions. Moreover, their lightweight nature simplifies construction processes and reduces transportation costs. The electronics and electrical sectors find applications for peanut-shell-powder-derived biocarbon, which can be used for manufacturing super capacitors and electrodes Ekpenyong, N.E.; Ekong, S.A.2023

The industrial applications of peanut-shell-powder composites are extensive and span across the automotive, packaging, construction, furniture, electronics, agriculture, aerospace, and sports sectors. Their unique combination of mechanical properties, sustainability, and versatility makes them a promising material choice for various industrial applications. Wei, X.; Wan, S.; 2015 ORANGE PEEL The orange peel has been processed through various approaches for using in foods, drugs, and cosmetics (Chen *et al.,* 2013).

Apart from being a good source of dietary fibers, orange peel extracts are a good source of biologically active compounds such as flavonoids and phenolic acids, which provides antioxidant, anti-carcinogenic, anti-inflammatory, and anti-atherosclerosis properties (Chen *et al.,* 2017). Orange peel, a common waste product, contain insoluble fibers (cellulose, hemicellulose, and lignin), and soluble fibers (pectin) (Pandiarajan *et al.,* 2018).

Additionally, orange peels also consist of essential oils and various bioactive compounds such as limonene, α-farnesene, γ-terpinene, myrcene, α-pinene, β-pinene, α- terpinolene etc., which provides antioxidant and antibacterial properties (Terzioğlu *et al.,* 2021).

Orange peels contain compounds such as pectin and essential oils, which could potentially be harnessed for their antimicrobial properties and ability to extend the shelf life of certain food products. Different extraction methods are used to extract natural products from orange peels. These methods include steam distillations, cold pressing, soxhlet extractions, solvent extractions, high pressure extractions, supercritical CO2 extractions, etc. (Rehan *et al.,* 2018)

While these methods are advantageous, they also have certain drawbacks such as long extraction times, high temperatures, incomplete extraction processing, and degradation of bioactive compounds. Thus, various emerging extraction techniques are used to extract bioactive compounds or biopolymers from orange peel such as extraction of pectin from orange peel using microwave assisted extraction (Maran *et al.,* 2013),

Extraction of metabolites using ultrasonic assisted emulsification method , etc. By using these new methods, active compounds can be extracted in a simple, rapid, and inexpensive manner The extracts of orange peel are used in developing food packaging. The active food packaging has also been developed using chitosan, poly vinyl alcohol, and, D-limonene, where, D-limonene is a cyclic terpene obtained in natural citrus oils (Lan *et al.,* 2020).

Moreover, orange peels have gained remarkable attraction to be used as bio filler materials for the fabrication of bio composites for packaging application. Additionally, there has been growing interest in using the available low-valued by-products such as orange peel in developing biocomposites as natural additions to increase the properties of composite films for targeted food packaging materials (Terzioğlu *et al.,* 2021)

This biofiller has the noteworthy attributes of abundancy, cost-effective, and biodegradability, and it has the potential to significantly improve value-added and ecologically friendly structural composites made from waste. Moreover, orange peel is considered a potential source of cellulose due to its high cellulose content, which can be used for various industrial applications, such as biodegradable packaging (Yaradoddi *et al.,* 2022)

The waste orange peels can be effectively used to extract cellulose nano crystals (CNCs) and other types of nano celluloses also, which in turn can be incorporated into polymer matrix to create nano composite films with enhanced properties. This process not only adds value to agricultural waste but also contributes to the development of sustainable materials for various industrial applications. CNCs have unique properties, such as high strength, lightweight, and biodegradability, making them ideal for various applications, including nano composites films. The biodegradable nature of CNC-based films offers an eco- friendly alternative to conventional plastics, aligning with global sustainability goals (Bigi *et al.,* 2023).

Further, in 2021, Othman & Fadzil reviewed the preparation and characterization of orange peels to be used as a commercial plastic against synthetic plastics, made from petroleum-based resources. Further, this orange peel waste is rich in bioactive compounds like pectin and cellulose, holds potential for bioplastic production and can also be used as a reinforcing agent for developing composites The incorporation of OP (orange peel) fillers into LLDPE can enhance the properties of the composite films. The optimal characteristics improve thermal stability, mechanical strength, and UV-blocking capabilities, while, reducing issues such as air bubble formation and particle agglomeration. OP fillers could be viable and can be used as a sustainable alternative to non-renewable resources in food packaging applications (Fehlberg *et al.,* 2020).

The integration of orange peel biowaste into composite films paves the way for their utilization in the active packaging field, offering a sustainable alternative to synthetic counterparts Utilizing orange peel waste has the potential to minimize the detrimental consequences associated with waste disposal, thereby fostering environmental sustainability. Orange peel waste is extensively used in food industry for developing bakery products, confectionery and beverages In this regard, the use of orange peel waste-based polymer composite for food packaging. orange peel powder and poly vinyl alcohol based biocomposite film for food packaging (Rathinavel & Saravanakumar, 2021)

Orange oil loaded pectin films as antibacterial material for food packaging cellulose nanofibers (CNF) derived from orange peel waste, orange peel waste based natural extractives, and poly(vinyl alcohol) based active food packaging orange peel waste based plastic for biodegradable packaging (Marsi *et al.,* 2019);

Orange peel extracts incorporated in PLA films for developing active food packaging biowaste orange peel reinforced chitosan and polyvinyl alcohol based composite for active packaging (Terzioğlu *et al.,* 2021) . Moreover, chitosan/polyvinyl alcohol composite films enriched with orange peel exhibit improved functional properties, making them suitable for sustainable and effective food packaging solutions. These eco-friendly films not only utilize agricultural waste but also offer enhanced protection and preservation for food products. Incorporation of orange peel powder enhanced barrier properties, flexibility, thermal stability, light protection, and antioxidant activity, which can help in extending the shelf life and maintaining the quality of packaged food items (Terzioğlu *et al.,* 2021).

Orange peels are the outer protective layer of the orange fruit, which is a valuable byproduct generated in the orange processing industry. Additionally, the components in orange peel have several health benefits being a noteworthy source of bioactive components, antioxidants and dietary fiber (Tahir *et al.,* 2023).

CONCLUSION

The review focus on agro waste by-products that are rich in bioactive compounds such as flavonoids, polyphenols, carotenoids, dietary fiber, and essential oils. These compounds contribute to its strong antioxidant, antimicrobial, anti-inflammatory, and anti-carcinogenic properties, making it a valuable natural ingredient. In the food industry, orange peel powder has been explored as a functional additive, offering improved nutritional value, flavor enhancement, and natural preservation properties due to its ability to inhibit microbial growth. In pharmaceuticals, its bioactive components have been linked to potential health benefits, including cholesterol reduction, improved digestion, and immune system support. Additionally, the cosmeticsindustry has leveraged orange peel powder for its skin-brightening, anti-aging, and exfoliating properties in skincare formulations. Beyond these applications, its role in sustainable waste management is gaining attention, as it can be repurposed for biodegradable packaging, natural dyes, and eco-friendly cleaning products.

REFERENCES

1. Varghese, S. A., Pulikkalparambil, H., Promhuad, K., & Harnkarnsujarit, N. (2023). Renovation of agro-waste for sustainable food packaging: A review. *Polymers*, 15(3), 648.
2. Birania, S., Kumar, S., Kumar, N., Attkan, A. K., & Kumar, V. (2021). Advances in development of biodegradable food packaging material from agricultural and agro-industry waste. *Journal of Food Process Engineering*, 45(8), e13930.
3. Mhaske, S. T., Mohanty, J. D., & Borse, P. Y. (2024). Starch from agro-waste for food packaging applications. In *Agro-Waste Derived Biopolymers and Biocomposites* (Chapter 9). Wiley.
4. Jain, A., Sarsaiya, S., Gong, Q., & Shi, J. (2024). Bioresources from biowaste for advancing manufacturing of packaging materials with modern circular economy towards a sustainable approach. *Environmental Development and Sustainability*.
5. Liu, Y., Ahmed, S., & Anjum, N. (2023). Turning agricultural waste into packages for food: A literature review from origin to end-of-life. *Environmental Technology & Innovation*, 30, 100143.
6. Salama, E., Mansy, A., Tian, Z.-Y., & Ossman, M. (2024). Effective decontamination of DR-81 dye from aqueous solutions using eco-friendly graphene oxide nanoparticles. *Environmental Science and Pollution Research*, 31, 12345–12358
7. Ahmad, A., Dubey, P., Younis, K., & Yousuf, O. (2022). Mosambi (Citrus limetta) peel and sago based biodegradable film: Development and characterization of physical, water barrier and biodegradation properties. *Journal of Food Science and Technology*, 59(3), 1234–1242.
8. Wypij, M., Trzcińska-Wencel, J., Golińska, P., & Rai, M. (2023). The strategic applications of natural polymer nanocomposites in food packaging and agriculture: Chances, challenges, and consumers' perception. *Environmental Research*, 214, 113851.
9. Kumari, S., Debbarma, R., Nasrin, N., & Bhuyan, T. (2024). Recent advances in packaging materials for food products. *Food Science and Technology*, 44, e12345.

CHAPTER 8

FOOD COLOURS -SYNTHETICS VS NATURAL

Anshida N and Safa
Department of Food Science and Nutrition, Nehru Arts and Science College, Coimbatore, Tamil Nadu-641 105

INTRODUCTION

Food coloring affects consumers in a number of ways. A more vivid color enhances the food's sensory appeal and promotes preference because it is closely related to the product's quality, vitality, and even nutritional makeup . These artificial colors, however, have no nutritional value and are only used for the special purpose of increasing sales. Numerous studies show that artificial coloring is directly linked to a number of medical disorders, including food allergies, cancer, and respiratory and gastrointestinal issues. Additionally, behavioral alterations in children are discussed, with children with autism spectrum disorder (ASD) being among the most affected by these challenges. (Li-Tung Huang and Nicola Magnavita, May 27, 2024)

Every food product is automatically examined visually before being purchased or consumed. Color is still one of the most noticeable visual indicators that contributes to the sensory experience of food. Numerous studies have demonstrated that food color psychologically influences our expectations of flavor before we even taste it. The majority of synthetic food colorants contain dyes from the azo group and are made from chemicals derived from coal tar compounds (Dey and Nagababu2022). Additionally, there are natural and synthetic colors that are identical, such as riboflavin (Varghese R and Ramamoorthy S, 2023).

The widespread use of food coloring was encouraged by a significant increase in the demand for packaged foods. Almost all food items sold or manufactured by the food industry or a food selling outlet now have food coloring added to them, as do all packaged and processed food products sold in markets. In order to attract customers, food coloring agents are also used in prepared food, such as that found in restaurants and other small food-selling establishments. But it is important to address the health risks that these intriguing artificial colors have been shown to cause, especially in children . There have also been reports of colorants working in concert to raise the prevalence of allergies and asthma . Due to their harmful effects on aquatic life forms and their subsequent consumers in the food chain, many organic dyes are also considered micro pollutants in aquatic environments (Tkaczyk *et al.,* 2020).

India frequently uses azo dyes and other synthetic food coloring agents that are prohibited in developed nations as food ingredients . Azo dyes are toxic and contain one or more azo groups (-N=N-) in their chemical structures.

According to reports, tartrazine, a common azo dye, can have harmful effects on the liver, kidneys, lipid profiles, and behavior (Amin and Al-Shehri 2019).

Food coloring, also known as a color additive, is any dye or material that, when added to food, drinks, or beverages, produces color. Food coloring is used in both home cooking and commercial food production. In food technology, food colorants come in a variety of forms and are chemicals added to food matrices to maintain or improve the food product's sensory qualities, which can be impacted or lost during processing or storage, as well as to maintain the intended color appearance. Color is an essential component of food and beverages, and modern consumers consider this when choosing food products. Many artificial food coloring additives have been used more frequently in recent years to replace natural colors in order to achieve specific qualities like increased color stability, uniformity, high color intensity, and improved appearance (Yang *et al.,* 2019).

Synthetic food coloring has a number of economically significant advantages over natural coloring, including low cost, high color stability, and resistance to light and pH. The majority of synthetic food coloring chemicals contain an azo-group and are derived from coal tar. In addition to the excessive use of approved synthetic colors, a variety of foods and drinks on the market may contain some prohibited synthetic colors. Several studies have verified that artificial food coloring is a significant cause of food intoxication and can result in serious health issues.

Several food additives that were once widely used are now prohibited because of evidence of their negative effects, medium- and long-term toxicity, and high risk of health incidents (Tripathi *et al.,* 2018).

It is also unsafe to use approved synthetic colors continuously. It is known that using honor-permitted colors and using them at random can have a negative impact on both human and animal health. The development of precise, sensitive, accurate, and selective analytical techniques for food analysis and quantification is necessary due to the use of food colorants in food production (Dey S and Nagababu B, 2019).

The industry prefers synthetic colorants, which are chemically or physically altered products with desirable manufacturing properties like high purity, coloring capacity, stability, brightness, a wide range of shades, production uniformity and reproducibility, and low cost in comparison to natural colorants. As science has advanced, more artificial colors have been developed that are very stable and allow a wide range of colors, which has led to their increasing use in the food industry.

However, many of the synthetic compounds are for human use, and despite ongoing research, natural alternatives have gained popularity among consumers worldwide due to recent findings about the toxicity and adverse effects of some synthetic dyes. Additionally, extremely specific techniques and procedures have been developed to identify the presence of artificial food coloring in food, which also allows for the determination of the likelihood of medium- and long-term toxicity and side effects. According to research, consuming artificial colorings of the azo type (E102, E110, E122, E123, E124, and E129), primarily nitro derivatives, can lead to certain health issues. According to a 2008 European Parliament directive, foods that contain one or more of these color additives must be labeled with the name or E-number information and the warning that it "may have an adverse effect on activity and attention in children." The safety of tartrazine (E102), a lemon yellow colorant, is one of the most contentious colorants. It is used in candies, ice cream, cereals, soups, jellies, cakes, soft drinks, and other foods. Due to its interaction with human serum proteins, it has been shown to have mutagenic properties and to be associated with obsessive-compulsive disorders and hyperactivity in children. Recent research on mice administered tartrazine at ADI levels revealed increased DNA abnormalities, immunotoxin effects, lipid oxidation changes in biochemical markers in brain tissue, and renal disorders. Carmoisine (E122), allura red (E129), ponceau 4R (E124), and sunset yellow (E110), which are derived from aromatic compounds derived from petroleum, have all been linked to increased pro-inflammatory activity. These compounds also bind to the serum albumin of humans and cows. Amaranth (E123), a dye that gives foods like candies, ice cream, and drinks their red hue and is legal in the EU but illegal in the US because it causes cancer, has demonstrated a high genotoxic effect on human lymphocytes in culture (Novais C *et al.,* 2022).

Recently, there has been a greater focus on the toxicity of food additives, specifically azo-dyes. Usually, this class of colorants is made up of vibrant hues.

However, the primary issue that frequently restricts their use is the possibility of carcinogenicity following intestinal microbiota-induced azoreduction to carcinogenic metabolites . Although the production of these metabolites in the human body is known, the phenomenon's clinical significance is contingent upon the quantity of colorant consumed .

Health issues due to synthetic food colorants

There are differing opinions on the health risks associated with food coloring because not all artificial food coloring is bad for humans. However, synthetic food coloring has been shown to have negative effects on human behavior, including hyperactivity, behavioral disorders, and attention deficits in children. This is likely due to the azo-benzene compound found in most synthetic food coloring, which is shown by their structures above and affects the majority of vital organs, genes, and metabolic processes. The presence of diazotizedsulfanilic acid and phenolic sulfonic acid moiety, which contain undesirable by-products from corresponding impurities, is the link between the structure of the synthetic colorants under discussion and their potential health risks. Sahar and Manal's study examined the effects of using food coloring (Colour fruit juice for 6–12 hours) on the biochemical levels of serum and the kidney and liver of rats over a 13-week period. Normal LDL cholesterol (TC) and triacyl-glycerol (TG) increased dramatically after eating tomato ketchup potato chips, as confirmed by TKPC (30%). The growth of rats given colored fruit juice (for 12 hours) and TKPC was significantly altered by the levels of Alanine Transaminase (ALT) and Aspartate Transaminase (AST), with TKPC being at 30%.

The levels of albumen and serum creatinine also increased significantly. Liver glutathione (GSH) was significantly reduced in both low and excessive consumption of colored foods. The study also demonstrated that the immune system's response to inflammation is correlated with an increase in red to white blood cell concentrations of color ingredients. Their results demonstrated that fruit juice containing carnosine, tartrazine, and sundown yellow raises the ALT of serum rats. Therefore, they concluded that the artificial colours used in their studies have detrimental effects on a number of the serum biochemical, liver and kidney. These effects were well-supported by research showing that rats given excessive amounts of artificial coloring (Tartrazine, Camosine, Sunset Yellow, and Fast Green) showed significantly higher serum ALT and AST levels than control rats. Increases in serum ALT and AST levels could also indicate hepatocellular impairment of intracellular enzymes in the blood, which would explain those changes in liver function. Histopathological studies made it clear. At low dose artificial colour, the liver showed a disruption of hepatic cells close to the vital vein and hepatocellular damage. According to an Okafor et al. report, artificial colors can have a harmful effect on vital organs. The degree and type of damage caused by the administration of the toxic compound determine whether a typically excessive stage of specific tissue enzymes is released into the bloodstream. Serum creatinine levels have also significantly increased. The impairment of renal interest is thought to be directly related to the exceptionally high creatinine stage elevation. When rats were given oral doses of azo dye (fast green) for thirty-five days, their serum creatine and urea levels significantly increased.

A significant increase in triglycerides was observed in the class of rats given chocolate and candy colored at both low and high concentrations. Furthermore, these effects are based on the findings of Floriano *et al.,* who found that rats given artificial coloring (tartrazine) and chocolate colors A and B that contain tartrazine and carnosine had significantly higher serum triglycerides.(*Et al.,* Uchegbu 2020)

The coloring qualities, consistency, stability, and affordability of synthetic dyes make them popular. Long-term use of many of them, however, can make them toxic, leading to health issues like indigestion, anemia, and allergic reactions like urticaria and asthma; pathological lesions in the brain, kidney, spleen, and liver; tumors and cancer; paralysis; mental retardation; abnormalities in offspring; growth retardation; and eye defects that result in blindness (Ashida *et al.,* 2000; Moutinho *et al.,* 2007). To enhance the visual appeal of the food products, several chemical food coloring agents are frequently added during processing .A study by McCann et al.concluded that, exposure to two mixtures of four synthetic colors plus the preservative sodium benzoate in the diet results in an increased hyperactivity in 3-year-old and 8- to 9-year-old children in the general population. While the most recent study by Moutinho has demonstrated that, tartrazine does not have a potential to induce benign or malignant neoplasias (Wahab H and Moram G, 2020).

Food poisoning could result from adulterations. Food illness, fatalities, and even adulterations of synthetic food colors are more likely to occur, especially in youngsters.

According to a number of studies Market-available items like bakery goods, confections, and beverages commonly incorporate artificial food coloring. Market-available foods and beverages may have both an excessive amount of legal artificial colors as well as certain prohibited synthetic colors.

Synthetic food colors have been linked to serious health issues likeallergies, low hemoglobin levels, genetic abnormalities, irritability, restlessness, effects on the organs, and, hyperactivity in children (KS & KJ, 1994; Tuormaa, n.d.). Pet food frequently comes in a spectrum of hues, and this is no accident. It's pleasant to see the golden chicken, and the scarlet of rare steak, when you unzip a package since these colors represent the original components" colors, which may lose during the production process. These colors are added after the event. The colors are actually included to attract pet parents because dogs and cats can't see the same range of hues that humans can. The use of these harmful food colors was outlawed by the Food and Drugs Act of 1906. Colors are frequently added to hide rotting or discoloration of food. Even though some food dyes, especially when used in large quantities, might well have cancer-causing effects, are not currently among the colors that the FDA has approved. FDA-approved colors should be harmless in foods for both people and pets if they are used as directed (Spence *et al.,* 2010). Animals exposed to semi-toxic concentrations of Sunset blue experience abnormalities in their body's overall lipid storage. This would have an impact on their metabolism and could result in dangerous liver damage including necrosis (Shalini Saxena, 2023)

Synthetic food colours have been increasingly used than natural food colours by food manufacturers to attain certain properties such as low cost, improved appearance, high colour intensity, more colour stability, and uniformity. Varied foods and beverages available in the market may contain some non-permitted synthetic colours and overuse of permitted synthetic colours. It may lead to severe health problems such as mutations, cancers, reduced haemoglobin concentrations, and allergic reactions. Therefore, there is a high tendency to use synthetic food colours in confectioneries and beverages and some confectioneries contain unidentified colours including a textile dye. Hence, the implementation of regulations and awareness programs of food colours for consumers and food manufacturers are highly recommended On the other hand, synthetic colors, produced from coal and petroleum, could be harmful. Synthetic colours are added to foods to replace natural colour lost during processing, to reduce batch-to-batch variation and to produce products with consumer appeal where no natural colour exists. Thus colouration of food allows the desired esthetic quality of a particular product, and for this reason it is of importance to food industries. Several sociological, technical and economic factors have influenced the food industry over the past two decades. The food market has changed rapidly with a much large proportion of foods being "processed" to meet the needs of new consumer segments. Hence food industry strives to provide visually appealing foods that have good taste and meet the consumers demand on quality and price. The demand for natural colours for food processing is increasing, mostly due to concerns about health risks triggered by some synthetic additives that can be toxic at metabolic, Physiological and toxicological levels. Synthetic dyes are widely used due to their coloring properties, uniformity, stability and low cost. However, many of them become toxic after prolonged use, causing health problems such as indigestion, anemia and allergic reactions as asthma and urticaria, pathological lesions in the brain, kidney, spleen and liver, tumors and cancer paralysis, mental retardation, abnormalities in Offsprings, growth retardation and eye defects resulting in blindness. Considering, among others, genotoxic and carcinogenic risks, urticaria, asthma, nausea, eczema, bronchitis, bronchitis, bronchospasm, headache, reduced blood coagulation and hyperactivity are some of the health issues (Kolkar K *et al.,* 2022).

Our daily diets now include unhealthy processed foods. The use of illegal food dyes, particularly synthetic ones, as coloring agents with genotoxic or carcinogenic qualities is common in these foods, raising concerns about public health. Over the past 50 years, the amount of artificial food dye consumed has multiplied, with children being the largest consumers. Some dyes may contain cancer-causing contaminants. Food dyes such as Erythrosine, Carmoisine, and Tartrazine are the leading causes of liver carcinogenesis. Azo dyes and triphenylmethanes are the most common classes of illegally added food dyes. The toxic activity of Azo dyes, which are widely used in industry, is a result of their metabolism. The enzyme-mediated Azo reduction leads to the formation of active aromatic amines attacking DNA. In this context, although they are still widely used, synthetic food colorants, due to their potential hazards, are being replaced by those obtained from natural origins.

Indeed, numerous side effects and toxicities, at both the medium and long-terms-namely allergic reactions, and behavioural and neurocognitive effects--have been related to the use of synthetic colorants (Malabadi R *et al.,* 2022).

The colouring additives applied to food products play an important role in consumers' preferences. However, their preferences for naturally derived colors which are closely associated to the image of healthy, safe and good-quality products sharply increased, as a large number of synthetic dyes have recognized side effects on human health. Accordingly, to overcome these constraints, new and specific sources and procedures must be recognized in order to improve not only the stability of food colouring additives and the final attractiveness of enriched-foodstuffs during the processing and storage practices but also their safety. The use of food colourants must be performed within the limits and to fulfill a certain function (Silva Met al,2022).

synthetic food colors have been increasingly used than natural food colors by food manufacturers to attam certain properties such as low cost, improved appearance, high color intensity, more color stability and uniformity. Varied foods and beverages available in the market may contain some non-permitted synthetic colors and over use of permitted synthetic colors. This may lead to severe health problems such as mutations, cancers, reduced hemoglobin concentrations and allergic reactions. Moreover, 60% of the beverages violated the label requirement without including proper color ingredients. Various factors that effect on human health include; the most concerning claim about artificial food dyes is that they cause cancer.

However, the evidence to support this claim is weak. Based on the research currently available, it is unlikely that consuming food dyes will cause cancer. Certain food dyes because allergic reactions in some people, but if you do not have anysymptoms of an allergy, there is no reason to eliminate them from your diet. The claim about food dyes that has the strongest science to back it up is the connection between food dyes and hyperactivity in children. Several studies have found that food dyes increase hyperactivity in children with and without The reason dyes are used in foods is to make food look more attractive. There is absolutely no nutritional benefit of food dyes.

The biggest sources of food dyes are unhealthy processed food that have other negative effects on health. Food dyes are likely not dangerous for most people, but avoiding processed foods that contain dyes can improve your overall (Dey S and Nagababu B, 2019)

Natural Food Colorant

Natural food colours or biological pigments originate from a wide range of sources like vegetables, fruits, plants, minerals and other edible natural sources.

These natural pigments are essential secondary metabolites, which play multiple roles in the whole life cycle of plants and are characterized by powerful medicinal properties. Owing to their nutritional benefits and phytochemicals, they are considered as functional food ingredients, capable of providing additional health benefits, like prevention or delaying onset of chronic diseases, as well as meeting basic nutritional requirements. Plant natural pigments plays an important role in plant metabolism and visual attraction in nature. Plant pigments are important clues to humans and animals in identifying the plant and plant parts such as leaf, fruit, flower, seed, root, and tubers.

Pigments are responsible for imparting colours to various plant parts. In fact, almost all plant parts are bound to be pigmented right from germination to their senescence.

Traits of the colours are thus a prerequisite for breeding programmes for developing coloured varieties. Colours are of prime importance for indicating diversity among genotypes for selecting elite parents during breeding programmes. Colour development is the most fascinating and complex phenomenon during ripening and is mainly governed by pigments. Colour is considered to be the first sensory perception of fruit, contributing to the commercial value of fruit because it attracts consumers.

Colour is an important characteristic and selection criterion for food choice. Recent studies have highlighted this importance and have shown how selection of colours may change among certain populations over a period of time (Chalannavar R*et al.,* 2022).

Naturally derived colorants are usually less stable to heat, light, and oxygen. They may interact with other ingredients, resulting in the development of unwanted colors and flavors. Naturally derived colors are usually less vivid. An appealing feature of natural colorants is that many may provide health benefits. Alternative color systems do not exist for all hues, e.g., FD&C Blue Number 1. Most of these challenges can be met with careful product design and testing. Also, it may be necessary to modify packaging and/or shorten product shelf life. The Natural Food Colours Associationhas suggested extending the EU definition of natural flavor to food colors. It is unlikely, however, that a global definition of natural color will be adopted in the near future because of the lack of consensus on how consumers interpret the term Replacement of artificial food dyes with natural colorants is a current marketing trend, notwithstanding the fact that neither the United States nor the European Union (EU) has defined natural with respect to food colors. Consumer groups have concerns over the safety of synthetic colorants, and in addition, many of the naturally derived colorants provide health benefits. Food scientists frequently have the assignment of replacing artificial colorants with natural alternatives. This can be challenging, as naturally derived colorants are usually less stable, and all desired hues might, in fact, not be obtainable (Wrolstad R, and Culver C, 2017).

For food color additives to be considered natural they should exist in nature and should contain natural raw materials. They may be derived from plant, animal, mineral or microbial sources and the chromophore should not be modified chemically during extraction or manufacturing. In some jurisdictions, a special category termed "nature identical" is recognized for chemically synthesized substances that are of identical chemical structure to natural pigments. Lists of natural colorants in use are long and variable among countries. Most natural colorants can be grouped into the following categories: carotenoids, anthocyanins, betains, caramel coloring, a wide variety of fruit juices, annatto, carmine, lycopene, paprika, turmeric, and saffron. Blue colors are especially rare in nature, but a blue pigment obtained from the Gardenia jasminoides plant is currently approved for use in Japan and a blue pigment extracted from the algae Spirulina platensis is also approved for use in many countries. Many publications on natural food colorants mention that evolving (or modern) consumer preferences and eating desires favor natural over synthetic colorants. This increased use of natural food colorants has been influenced by some purported associations between the intake of synthetic colorants and exacerbation of some conditions, such as attention deficit and hyperactivity in children, and allergies, in sensitive subpopulations. However, despite scientific expert evaluations concluding on their safety and continued regulatory approval, the public concerns about synthetic Tood colorants remain and are an influential force in shaping current market trends toward colors from natural sources. Consumer interest in natural colorants is also Influenced by health benefit claims that are published in the scientific and layliterature. Therefore, Industry is actively pursuing the development of new natural colors and new applications for existing natural colors despite cost and stability considerations Contemporary efforts to address cost and stability concerns include investigating various technological options, such as microencapsulation and nano formulations, use of carrier materials, sequestrants and antioxidants to reduce color loss, and improved processing and packaging. Biotechnological development of natural colorants using cell cultures and using filamentous and marine fungi as colorant sources are being investigated to address production costs. Microbial pigments can be produced in large quantity at relatively low cost compared b extraction from plants (Maronport R *et al.,* 2020).

Plant pigments should be used to replace pigment lost during processing, since they are essentially the same compounds as those contained in the original or similar plant material and have a long history of consumption extending over thousands of years. A 'natural colour' can be defined as a colour extracted from a plant or animal source, in such a manner that the pigments remain chemically unchanged. A 'nature-identical colour, on the other hand, is one that is synthesized from chemical feedstocks so that it is structurally identical to pigments occurring in nature. They can be divided conveniently into several groups, such as flavonoids (largely anthocyanins), carotenoids, chlorophylls, betalaines, and others (curcumin and carthamin). EEC numbers have been given to the colours as aids to consumer identification (Timberlake C.F and Henry, 2020).

There has been much interest in the development of new natural colorants for use in the food industry, which is apparently due to strong consumer demand for more natural products, at least in some countries. There is no doubt that it is technologically Teasible to prepare new natural colorants from locally known plants or microorganisms that have not yet been investigated scientifically. However, on considering economic, legislative and consumer acceptance aspects, prospects for new food colorants look less promising. It is unlikely that it will be possible to introduce completely new natural colorants into today's food manufacturing industry, as long as current food legislation and consumer attudes remain unchanged Wissgott U and Bortik.K, 2021).

Naturally occurring color additives that were sourced from vegetables and minerals were used in ancient times, while the first artificially colored food was wine, back in 300 BCE. In 1856, Wilian Perkin discovered mauve, the first synthetic dye, sourced from coal, creating a trend of coal-tar-colors. In the United States (US), the federal government started regulating food dyes back in the 1880s, and allowed dyes that were quite harmful to human health, although at the time, technology was not enough to understand this harm. In 1927, when the control and regulation of food dyes, as well as all food additives was handed over to the Food and Drug Administration of the United States of America, which until today enforces control over food related issues. Today, some food additives have, in the US, a special authorization known as GRAS - Generally Regarded as Safe, meaning their use in amounts enough to fulfill their intended function is safe, but, in food colorants, no additive if considered GRAS. This is due to the sources of food additives, which in some cases are toxic, thus needing proper regulation (Durazza A *et al.,* 2022).

On supermarket shelves the proliferation of products with labels that make a virtue of "No artificial colours suggests that the future of the azo dyes and their various chemical cousins is strictly limited. Nature makes an abundance of colours and many of these are extracted and used as natural food colorants, however, they are subject to application limitations and stability problems. Significant research is ongoing by academia and industry into methods to stabilise and expand the application possibilities for the various approved natural food colorants, but most developments that the food colour manufacturers boast about nowadays are enhanced vehicles for delivering established natural pigments into food (Blackburn R and Coultate T, 2020).

Health benefits of Natural food colorants

Natural food colourants (biocolorants) may also play an important role in human health as they contain some biologically active compounds, which possess a number of pharmacological properties like strong antioxidant, antimutagenic, anti-inlammatory and antiartheritic effects Carotenoids are also used as vitamin supplements, since -carotene is the precursor of vitamin A. The regular intake of carotene can help prevent night blindness resulting from inadequate supply of vitamin A. Carotenoids also act as biological antioxidants, protecting cells and tissues from the damaging effects of free radicals and singlet oxygen and also as a good source of anti-tumor agent Lycopene, is particularly effective at quenching the destructive potential of singlet oxygen. Lutein, zeaxanthin and xanthophylls are believed to function as protective antioxidants in the macular region of the human retina. These compounds also act against aging, mascular degeneration, and senile cataracts. Canthaxanthin also shows antioxidant property. Astaxanthin is another naturally occurring xanthophyll with potent antioxidant properties (Okafor S*et al.,*2021)

Other health benefits of biocolorants include enhancement of immune system function, protection from sunburn, and inhibition of the development of certain types of cancers. Lycopene prevents oxidation of low-density lipoprotein (LDL) cholesterol and reduces the risk of developing atherosclerosis and coronary heart disease. Epidemiological studies have revealed a correlation between the consumption of chlorophylls and decreased risk of colon cancer. They have also been observed to possess antineoplastic, radiation-protective, vasotonic, vasoprotective, anti-inflammtory and hepatoprotective activities. A flavaoured and brightly coloured seed of Manikara obovate has been showed to have both antioxidant and hepatoprotective activities (Obonga W*et al.,* 2019)

The natural colorants in natural plants have been the source of the traditional colorants of raw as well as the processed food. Betalains are water-soluble, nitrogen containing plant pigments present in most plants of the order Caryophylales. Betalains are distributed not only in edible parts of plants but also in flowers, leaves, stem and bracts. These are classified into two groups,violetbetacyanins and the yellow befaxanthins. Both groups shared betalamic acid as the structural and chromophoric unit. Betalains are water-soluble, nitrogen containing plant pigments present in most plants of the order Caryophyllales. Betalains are distributed not only in edible parts of plants but also in flowers, leaves, stem and bracts. These are classified into two groups, violet betacyanins and the yellow betaxanthins. Chlorophyls are oil soluble and the most widespread distributed pigments responsible for the Characteristic green color of plants. The structure of chlorophylls is porphyrins or tetrapyroles chelated with a centrally located magnesium atom. The main chlorophylls in foods are chlorophyll a and chlorophyll b. Chlorophylls are highly sensitive to heat, light, oxygen, acids and enzymes, leading to their prompt degradation and color change. Carotenoids are plant pigments with 40 carbon atoms molecule. Carotenoids have provitamin A activity because the body can convert them into retinol. Carotenoids are lipid soluble, yellow-orange red pigments found in all higher plants and some animals. Carotenoids can be classified into carotenes containing only carbon and hydrogen, and xanthophylls made up of carbon, hydrogen, and oxygen. It is more stable at pH between 4.0 and 6.0.

Degradation of carotenoids is mainly occurs due to reactions of oxidation and isomerization, which tend to a decrease in the redness and yellowness of a plant pigments. Anthocyanins are water soluble plant pigments. They are responsible for the blue, purple, red and orange colors of many fruits and vegetables. They occur mainly as glycosides of their respective aglycone anthocyanidin chromophores with the sugar moiety generally attached at the 3-position on the C-ring or the 5- position on the A-fing. Only six antocyanidin are common namely, cyanidin, delphinidin, petunidin, Peonidin, pelargonidin, and malvidin which are widely spread and of great importance in human diet and health (Jadhav R and Buibal S, 2020). Nowadays, due to the difficulties in controlling the origin of food and the genered rend of the word in the use of natural products, the studies on the otracion of natural food colorings are increasingly attracting the attention of ecientists. As a result, the studies on the extraction of natural food colorings have greatinterest. Since ancient times, humans have known the use of food colorings from nature. According to moder science, natural food colorings, particularly from fruits and vegetables, are generated mainly as four groups of pigments: the green chlorophylls, the yellow-orange-red carotenoids, the red-blue-purple anthocyanins, and the red betanin (Gia Hanle *et al.,* 2018).

The natural color of foods is due primarily to carotenoids, anthocyanins, betanin and chlorophylls, either as inherent food constituents or as food or feed additives.

These compounds have drawn considerable attention in recent years, not because of their coloring properties, but due to their potential health-promoting effects. Their occurrence and levels in foods, along with the factors that influence the composition, have been widely investigated. Processing effects have been actively studied. In spite of the intense search for plant and microbial sources and efforts to increase yield, few natural food color additives have reached the market (Della B Rodriguez-Amaya, 2020).

CONCLUSION

The use of food colours, whether synthetic or natural, remains an essential aspect of the modern food industry, primarily for improving product aesthetics, consumer appeal, and market competitiveness. Synthetic food colours have long been favored for their vibrant hues, stability, and cost-effectiveness; however, increasing health concerns linked to their consumption, including allergic reactions, hyperactivity, and potential toxicological effects, have raised significant safety debates. These concerns have driven the food industry and consumers towards safer and more sustainable alternatives.

Natural food colours, extracted from plants, fruits, vegetables, algae, and other natural sources, not only provide attractive colouring properties but also offer added health benefits due to their bioactive compounds such as antioxidants, vitamins, and antimicrobial properties. Despite their advantages, natural colours face certain limitations including poor stability under heat, light, and pH variations, lower colouring intensity, and higher production costs, which restrict their large-scale industrial applications.Recent advancements in food technology, including microencapsulation, nanotechnology, and genetic engineering, offer promising solutions to overcome these challenges. The future of food colouring lies in the innovation and development of stable, cost-effective, and health-promoting natural colours. Ultimately, the transition from synthetic to natural food colours aligns with the growing consumer demand for clean-label, health-oriented, and environmentally sustainable food products.

REFERENCES

1. Coultate, T., & Blackburn, R. S. (2018). Food colorants: Their past, present and future. *Coloration Technology*, 134(3), 165–186.
2. Martins, N., Roriz, C. L., Morales, P., Barros, L., & Ferreira, I. C. F. R.

(2017). Coloring attributes of betalains: A key emphasis on stability and future applications. *Food & Function*, 8(4), 1357–1372.

3. Gulzar, T., & Benjakul, S. (2022). Natural food colorants: Extraction and stability study. *Materials Today: Proceedings*, 57(6), 2381–2395.
4. Rodrigues, S., & Fernandes, Â. (2024). A critical review on the stability of natural food pigments and stabilization techniques. *Food Research International*, 170, 112963.
5. Luzardo-Ocampo, I., Ramírez, A., Yañez, J., Mojica, L., & González de Mejía, E. (2021). Technological applications of natural colorants in food systems: A review. *Foods*, 10(3), 634.
6. Carocho, M., Morales, P., & Ferreira, I. C. F. R. (2017). Food colorants: Challenges, opportunities and current desires of agro-industries to ensure consumer expectations and regulatory practices. *Trends in Food Science & Technology*, 62, 141–153.
7. Siva, R., & Muthuchelian, K. (2017). Natural colorants: Historical, processing and sustainable prospects. *Natural Products and Bioprospecting*, 7(1), 123–145.
8. Downham, A., & Collins, P. (2000). Colouring our foods in the last and next millennium. *International Journal of Food Science & Technology*, 35(1), 5–22.
9. Delgado-Vargas, F., Jiménez, A. R., & Paredes-López, O. (2000). Natural pigments: Carotenoids, anthocyanins, and betalains—Characteristics, biosynthesis, processing, and stability. *Critical Reviews in Food Science and Nutrition*, 40(3), 173–289.
10. Sigurdson, G. T., Tang, P., & Giusti, M. M. (2017). Natural colorants: Food colorants from natural sources. *Annual Review of Food Science and Technology*, 8, 261–280.

CHAPTER 9

EDIBLE COATING FOR FRUITS FROM AGRO WASTE

Akash A V and RajaKumaran P

Department of Food Science and Nutrition, Nehru Arts and Science College, Coimbatore, Tamil Nadu-641 105

INTRODUCTION

Fruit consumption has increased over the past few decades, so fruit production has increased globally. However, fresh produce is prone to significant losses during production and preservation. Various technical treatments are applied to fruits to maintain their quality during the postharvest preservation stage. One widely used technology is the application of edible coatings, which can be applied to a variety of fruits to control the exchange of gases and moisture between the fruit and its surroundings. Additionally, edible coatings offer a significant advantage by allowing the integration of various active ingredients into the matrix of the coating, meaning that these substances will associate with and possibly be consumed with the fruit. The fruit's nutritional value, organoleptic properties, and shelf life would all be enhanced by this. An overview of the data on common coating matrix components is given in this paper, with an emphasis on how material combinations and application methods affect fruit qualities. With this information, processors may select the right coating substance and concentration for a variety of fresh and fresh-cut fruits. The limitations and recent advancements in the use of edible coatings to extend the shelf life of fruits are also reviewed in this research(Pham *et al.,* 2023).

Hydrocolloids, or water-soluble gums, have a wide range of uses as thickeners, stabilizers, emulsifiers, texture modifiers, coating agents, and packaging films. The main purpose of edible coatings is to improve the appearance of food items and prolong the fruits' shelf life. Natural gums like chitosan, alginate, xanthan, gellan, mesquite, psyllium, basil seed, guar, tragacanth, and arabic gums have been shown in numerous studies to have the potential to be used in the development of edible coatings and to improve their qualities. Apple, papaya, carrot, guava, plum, mango, apricot, banana, orange, tomato, and mushroom quality and shelf-life were characterized using innovative biodegradable edible coverings based on natural gums. Longer shelf life, delayed ripening, reduced respiration rate, biocompatibility, environmental friendliness, affordability and good mass transfer barrier qualities are just a few advantages that the edible coatings made from natural gums may offer. They may also act as carriers of food additives like vitamins, antioxidants, and antimicrobials. To attain a significant decrease in the weight loss of fruits and vegetables, 20% glycerol (w/w) was added to edible coating solutions that contained 1% gum(Salehi, 2020).

The work investigated a new edible coating material with improved mechanical and gas barrier qualities by combining silk fibroin (SF) with poly(vinyl alcohol) (PVOH). SF and PVOH water suspensions were combined in varying ratios to form multilayered membranes that, after phase separation, formed on the surface of fresh-cut produce during dip coating. The effects of the mixing ratio on the film's transparency, mechanical characteristics, water vapor and oxygen permeability were examined. Higher PVOH fractions resulted in enhanced ductility (higher elongation at break and lower Young's modulus), which is required for food packaging materials. A coating with an SF:PVOH weight ratio of 1:1 demonstrated the lowest water vapor permeability and was chosen for perishable food preservation trials. After 14 days of storage at 4 °C, coated fresh-cut apples showed much less weight loss and colour change than uncoated controls. To create an active food coating with oxygen scavenging capabilities, ascorbic acid was also added to the coating material. The acquired results showed that SF:PVOH blends can form bilayered edible coatings that prolong the fresh-cut produce's shelf life(Ruggeri *et al.,* 2020).

EDIBLE COATING – PROMISING FUTURE

By the completion of harvest, climatic fruits continue to mature and release ethylene, and along with an increase in respiration rate, expedites perishability. It has been demonstrated that ethylene biosynthesis inhibition is an effective strategy for delaying the ripening process and extending shelf life. An effective method for maintaining the quality of fruits is the application of edible coatings. Using natural ingredients, being inexpensive, and being simple to apply are just a few advantages of edible coatings. Novel strategies for controlling fruit shelf life after harvest are offered by nanotechnology. Nanotechnology has the ability to create new materials by reducing component sizes to nanometric levels. When it comes to postponing fruit ripening and degradation, these nanomaterials have unique and enhanced qualities. Enhancing the mechanical and water vapor barrier qualities of the biopolymer is the primary objective of incorporating nanoparticles into edible coatings. In addition to having characteristics similar to biopolymers, nanoparticles are believed to possess better antiviral, antifungal, and antibacterial qualities than edible coatings. The purpose of this review is to provide an overview of current research on the use of edible coating in the form of nanoparticles and how they affect climacteric fruit quality metrics and shelf life extension. These days, chitosan nanoparticles, zinc, and silver are frequently utilized to cover climacteric fruits. It has been demonstrated that by lowering weight, moisture loss and maintaining fruit firmness, zinc nanoparticles are more effective in considerably postponing ripening(Odetayo *et al.,* 2022).

One of the most widely planted horticultural crops, tomatoes have a short shelf life because of their climacteric ripening, vulnerability to postharvest microbial deterioration, and mechanical injury, which causes significant postharvest losses. Using edible coatings to preserve tomato quality and extend its shelf life during storage has recently been viewed as a promising environmentally friendly and sustainable solution. The needs of edible coatings for whole fresh tomatoes are not expressly covered in any of the many publications that are available on the subject of edible coating for fresh produce, particularly tropical and stone fruits. In addition to summarizing or analysing the most recent research on the application of edible coating on tomatoes, this will provide the information about the desirable coating property needs unique to tomatoes. The study also discusses current developments in the application of bioactive chemicals and nanotechnological methods to enhance the functionality and performance of tomato coated materials. However, tomato edible coating technology is still in its infancy, and commercial technology adoption necessitates both widespread consumer acceptance and economic sustainability(Yadav *et al.,* 2022).

An excellent substitute to preserve and extend the fruits' shelf life are edible coatings made from natural ingredients. In order to extend the shelf life of fresh goldenberries, this study created edible coverings based on active carboxymethyl cellulose (CMC) and enhanced with beneficial chemicals that were isolated from spent coffee grounds (SCG). In order to compare the effects of three different treatments on fresh goldenberries, three different coatings were tested: (i) coating CMC (CMC-based edible coating); (ii) coating CMC-A (CMC-based edible coating with 0.2% (w/v) of polysaccharide-rich extract from SCG); and (iii) coating CMC-B (CMC-based edible coating with 0.2% (w/v) of polysaccharide-rich extract and 0.2% (w/v) of phenolic compounds encapsulated from SCG). The fruits' microbiological and physicochemical characteristics were assessed over the course of 12 and 28 days of storage at 4 °C and 95% relative humidity and 20 °C and 65% relative humidity, respectively. According to the findings, goldenberries' quality was greatly impacted by temperature and relative humidity, with storage at 4 °C and 95% RH nearly doubling their shelf life. Weight loss was managed and gas transfer rates (O2, CO2, and C2H4) were reduced by both CMCA and CMC-B coatings, primarily when goldenberries were kept at 20 °C and 65% relative humidity. Additionally, coating CMC-A was more effective at slowing down microbial growth, whereas coating CMC-B, which is edible and added phenolic compounds to goldenberries, enhancing their antioxidant capacity(Ballesteros *et al.,* 2022).

Derivatives of cellulose have been widely used as an edible coating for fruits and vegetables because of their affordability, availability, stability, solubility, and safety. Therefore, the purpose of this study was to: (1) extract cellulose from the rachis of the banana plant, (2) transform it into carboxymethyl (CMC), and (3) apply the resulting CMC as an edible covering to strawberry fruit in order to delay senescence and increase its shelf life. Using sodium hydroxide and monochloroacetic acid (MCA) in an etherification process with ethanol as a supporting medium, CMC was prepared. In order to characterize CMC, the FTIR spectra, degree of substitution (DS), ash content, CMC yield, water and oil holding capacity, and physical parameters were examined. The effect of

CMC as an edible covering on the shelf life of strawberry fruits was examined in a storage research. The production of food-grade CMC with high purity was accomplished. With a DS of 0.78, an oil holding capacity of 1.60 g/g, and a water holding capacity of 11.24 g/g, CMC demonstrated a yield of 156.25%. The resulting CMC worked well for making edible coatings and was used to extend the shelf life of strawberry fruits were kept at 22 °C to 6 days and those were kept at 4 °C to 16 days. Weight loss, pH, anthocyanin and ascorbic acid content, total soluble solids (TSS), decay percentage, firmness, and sensory qualities of strawberry fruit coated with CMC and kept at 4 °C were all better than those kept at 22 °C. To prevent postharvest senescence and preserve the quality of ambient and cold-stored fruits, CMC edible coating made from banana rachis may be suggested as a possible postharvest treatment(Abdullah *et al.,* 2023).

The market and demand for minimally processed fruits have grown globally in recent years. Apple browning is a result of fresh-cut apples' extraordinary sensitivity to external elements like oxygen, temperature, and microbes. Aloe vera and carboxymethyl cellulose were thus used to create varying concentrations of blended edible-coating solution in this investigation different ratio where used. The coating solution with 3% aloe vera and 2% carboxymethyl cellulose (CMC) had a typical particle size of 101.74 ± 0.67 nm. The apples' ten-day shelf life under refrigerated conditions was then assessed. The findings indicated that the weight loss of coated (6.42%–10.26%) and uncoated (8.12%–15.32%) apples over a period of two to ten days differed significantly. Additionally, over the course of storage, the chopped apples' titrable acidity rose. According to rheological data, the coating solution's viscosity falls as the temperature rises from 0 to 50°C. The existence of the hydroxyl group (-OH), C=O, C-O, and N-H bands in the A. vera, CMC, and blend-coating solution was verified by FTIR data. Excellent antibacterial efficacy was demonstrated by the blend solution. At day 0, the total phenolic content of coated and uncoated apples was 717.88 mg GAE kg^{-1} for the uncoated apple and 737.55 mg GAE kg^{-1} for the coated apple. However, compared to control apples, the aerobic and psychrotrophic bacterial populations for edible coated apples were much lower. The aerobic and psychrotrophic bacterial counts for coated apples were 1.59 ± 0.84 and 1.25 ± 0.49 log CFU g^{-1} at day 10, respectively, and 4.26 ± 0.67 and 2.68 ± 0.22 log CFU g^{-1}, respectively. In summary, a combination of A. vera and CMC may be utilized as a nontoxic, possible anti-browning, and antibacterial ingredient to extend the shelf life and provide nutritional value to fresh-cut apples(Tosif *et al.,* 2023).

Bamboo cellulose's high strength-weight ratio and biodegradability have made it a popular choice for reinforcement for polymers or as a template material in the production of composites. Four extraction techniques—hydrothermal extraction (HT), standard alkali extraction (SA), ambient condition extraction (AC), and two-stage extraction (TS)—are examined in this work for their impact on the morphology, structure, and characteristics of bamboo cellulose. TS can produce pure cellulose I with intact single cell morphology and good crystallinity among various techniques. The cellulose recovered via SA exhibits exceptional toughness and thermal stability, mixed cellulose I and II structure, and full cell shape. In contrast, the cellulose that was extracted by HT contains hemicellulose residues. However, it performs better in terms of heat stability and mechanical qualities. Although AC has the advantage of producing pure cellulose I without the need for thermal history, the cellulose's morphology is damaged due to the lengthy treatment period(Lin *et al.,* 2021).

The high tensile strength, huge specific surface area, great biocompatibility, and renewability of cellulose nanocrystals (CNC) have led to their widespread use in a variety of fields. Cellulose is the foundation of CNC and is present in considerable concentrations in the majority of biomass wastes. The majority of biomass wastes are composed of forest residues, agricultural trash, etc. CNC can be made from biomass wastes by using mechanical techniques such as oxidation hydrolysis, enzymatic hydrolysis, and acid hydrolysis to remove the non-cellulosic components. Biomass wastes, on the other hand, are typically burned or disposed of carelessly, which has serious negative effects on the environment. The development of CNC-based carrier materials from biomass wastes is therefore a successful tactic to encourage the highvalue utilization of biomass wastes. The benefits of using CNC, the extraction procedure, and new developments in CNC-based composites, including films, metal complexes, hydrogels, and aerogels, are outlined in this paper. Additionally, a detailed discussion of the CNC-based material's drug release properties is given. We also talk about certain knowledge gaps and possible future paths for CNC-based materials(Liu *et al.,* 2023).

APPLICATION OF CELLULOSE IN BIODEGRADABLE PACKAGING

Applications of cellulose-based coatings for tropical fruits have garnered a lot of interest due to their good coating-forming qualities. Nevertheless, there aren't many reviews of how the mechanical coating affects tropical fruit. This article discusses cellulose-based coating materials, their synthesis and functional characteristics, how active agents are included into coating materials, and how coatings affect the quality of tropical fruit. Carboxymethyl cellulose's higher hydrophilicity makes it appropriate for tropical fruit coverings. The physical characteristics of the covering materials are essential for maintaining the quality of tropical fruits. Incorporating or encapsulating bioactive molecules into the coating material can improve its properties and utility by reducing the negative effects of physical, chemical, and microbiological elements(Bahmid *et al.,* 2024).

The by-product of agriculture-based enterprises, which are frequently abundant in lignocellulosic materials and bioactive chemicals, is agro-industrial waste. These wastes are frequently disposed of in uncontrolled ways due to inadequate regulations on their management by the industries. The ecosystem and the overall economy have suffered as a result of these activities. In order to recover useful molecules from these wastes, extensive study has been done as a result of this issue. With a variety of uses, cellulose derived from agro-industrial waste has emerged as a renewable resource. The chemistry, structure, and process for obtaining cellulose and nanocellulose from several agro-industrial waste sources are covered in this review paper. This paper also discusses some of the new and creative uses of cellulose and nanocellulose in food. The safety concerns around the use of nanocellulose in food applications are outlined in the second section of this review(Ahmad Khorairi *et al.,* 2023).

RECENT DEVELOPMENT

The focus of this study is the most recent developments in cellulose and its derivatives. We provide an overview of the traits, qualities, uses, and changes of cellulose. We talk about recent developments in modified cellulose that provide more control here. This review examines advancements in various methods used for cellulose and its derivatives in addition to conventional methods. The many approaches to synthetic polymers are also covered. Functional celluloses with improved physical properties can now be produced thanks to recent developments in polymer synthesis, which enable more exact control. Since cellulose is nature's most plentiful renewable resource, green processing has been developed to promote sustainability and environmental preservation. With the discovery of cellulose disintegration, new avenues for environmentally friendly methods arise. The analysis of contemporary scientific literature has led us to conclude that the introduction of extra chemical units of cellulose solubility is necessary. This analysis will assess the long-term sustainability of biomass and the greenness of processing. In addition to dissolution, it seems to be essential to any process's greenness(Aziz *et al.,* 2022).

Despite having strong networks of hydrogen bonds between their molecular chains, many polysaccharides, including cellulose, are resistant to aqueous solvents. Although it also examines cellulose's interactions with wood, cell wall production, dispersion in aqueous suspensions, and potential applications in natural and synthetic composites, this review focuses on cellulose's interactions with water. The notion that cellulose is amphiphilic is critically reviewed, with implications for its processing. Building on this, advancements in the stabilization of oil-water emulsions through the use of different charged and modified forms of nanocellulose are discussed. It discusses the part that water plays in the aqueous production of chiral nematic liquid crystals and their subsequent drying into composite films(Etale *et al.,* 2023).

The most abundant polysaccharide on Earth, cellulose is found in a wide variety of sources, including the cell walls of plants and wood, certain types of bacteria and algae, and tunicates, the only known animals that contain cellulose. This abundance naturally opens the door to the discovery of new uses for this versatile material. This review offers a thorough overview of cellulose and its derivatives, including their structural and biochemical properties, as well as an overview of applications in drug delivery systems, tissue engineering, and wound dressing. Based on the methods available for choosing the physical characteristics, dimensions, and shapes, cellulose comes in the morphological forms of fiber, microfibril/nanofibril, and micro/nanocrystalline cellulose. Despite having a wide range of potential applications, the extensive use of cellulose has been primarily limited to industrial use, with less early interest in the biomedical field. Therefore, this review highlights recent developments in the preparation methods of cellulose and its derivatives that create novel properties benefiting appropriate biomedical applications. These different cellulosic particle types arise either because of the inherent diversity among the source of organic materials or because of the specific conditions of biosynthesis and processing that determine the consequent geometry and dimension of cellulosic particles(Seddiqi *et al.,* 2021).

Agriculture is essential for satisfying the increasing global food requirements. Nonetheless, conventional agricultural methods frequently result in detrimental environmental effects, including soil erosion and chemical runoff. There is an urgent demand for advanced agricultural techniques. Cellulose-based mulches present a viable solution by enhancing agricultural productivity while reducing environmental impact. These mulches are produced from renewable bioresources sourced from cellulose-rich materials. In comparison to plastic mulches, cellulose-based alternatives demonstrate potential for improving nutrient retention, soil health, weed suppression, water conservation, and erosion control. The article examines the properties and application techniques of cellulose-based mulches, emphasizing their biodegradability, water retention, crop protection, and weed suppression capabilities. Additionally, it assesses their viability from an economic standpoint, highlighting their capacity to revolutionize sustainable farming methods. All things considered, cellulose-based mulches have the power to transform agriculture by resolving environmental issues and maximizing output. They are an important step in the direction of a more resilient and sustainable agriculture system(Saberi Riseh, 2024).

FUNCTIONAL APPLICATION OF GUGGUL GUM IN PACKAGING FILM

Guggul, also called bdellium in India, is a flowering plant that produces oleoresin and belongs to the Burseraceae family. It is primarily found in rocky areas of the world and possesses a wealth of chemical components, including lignans, triterpenoids, amino acids, sesquiterpenoids, steroids, and flavonoids. The leaves, roots, and stem extracts of this plant are used in medicine for a variety of ailments, including skin conditions, wound healing, anti-cancer, anti-inflammatory, anti-microbial activity, ulcers, snake bites, stomach pain, wound healing, and muscle relaxation.(Sultan *et al.,* 2023)

Using a free radical graft copolymerization process, we created guggul gumbased hydrogel (GgG-cl-poly(AA)) in this study. N, N′-methylenebisacrylamide was used as the crosslinker, acrylic acid as the monomer, and ammonium persulfate as an initiator in the preparation process. Reaction time, solvent volume, microwave power, crosslinker amount, initiator concentration, and monomer concentration were all optimized in order to fully examine the synthesised hydrogel's swelling capability and equilibrium swelling ratio. In an aqueous solution, the swelling findings showed that the synthesized hydrogel could achieve a maximum percentage swelling of 980% in about three hours. Nuclear magnetic resonance, scanning electron microscopy, X-ray diffraction, Fourier transform infrared, and thermogravimetric analysis were used to characterize the produced hydrogel sample. The produced hydrogel was evaluated for resistive swelling, water absorbance at room temperature, water retention behavior in the soil, and reswelling experiments in a range of salt solutions at varying pH levels and temperatures. Remarkably, in contrast to the water solutions, the crosslinked hydrogel exhibited a reduced capacity for swelling in all salt solutions. With a maximum biodegradation of 87.7% using the soil burial method and 95.65% using the vermicomposting method, the biodegradation tests were carried out in both methods for two months. Considering these results, the guggul gum-based crosslinked hydrogel appears to be a promising option for a range of agricultural uses(S. Saleem *et al.,* 2024).

When the stem bark of Commiphora wightii (Arnott) Bhandari is damaged, a pathological oleo-gum resin known as "guggul" is produced [syn. "Commiphora mukul (Hook. Ex Stocks) Engl; Balsamodendron mukul (Hook. Ex Stocks)"; Family: Burseraceae]. It grows natively in the arid, warm regions of Gujarat and Rajasthan in India, as well as in Pakistan's adjacent areas. In the Ayurvedic medical system, it has been used since ancient times to treat a wide range of conditions, such as lipid problems, inflammation, rheumatism, obesity, gout, bone fractures, and arthritis. Other terpenoids (di- and triterpenoids), sugars, lignans, flavonoids, guggultetrols, amino acids, and volatile oil (rich in terpenoidal components monoterpenoids and sesquiterpenoids) make up the majority of guggul resin. The chemical components, medicinal properties, and applications of this oleo-gum resin are all thoroughly described in this compilation. The IUCN Red List of Threatened Species includes Guggul, which has been designated as a Critically Endangered species. Nonscientific techniques of tapping and collecting resin, commercial exploitation, and poor plant regeneration are some of the main causes of its current state. In order to prevent the complete extinction of this essential medicinal plant, strict conservation efforts are necessary(Sarup *et al.,* 2022).

The physico-chemical and qualitative characteristics of jamun (Syzgium cumini L.) fruit were examined during storage at 20°C for 12 days in the presence of guggul gum (GG) at 5, 10, and 15% (w/v) enhanced with 0.1% basil oil (BO). GG 10% + BO 0.1% or GG 15% + BO 0.1% treated jamun fruit considerably decreased weight loss, decay incidence, and total soluble solids as compared to the control fruit. The same procedure hindered the activity of the enzymes polygalacturonase (PG) and cellulase (CEL) and postponed the depolymerization of the pectin content. Higher firmness, titratable acidity, ascorbic acid, phenolics, and overall antioxidant activity of jamun fruit were effectively maintained when BO was added to GG 10% or GG 15%. The results reveal that GG and BO may be a novel technique for delaying the physico-chemical changes and prolonging the shelf life of jamun fruit during storage. Additionally, the experts have not seen any adverse impacts of GG and BO on the sensory quality of jamun fruit(Khaliq *et al.,* 2020).

Commiphora mukul is a highly significant plant with a variety of medicinal uses. The Burseraceae family, which includes many therapeutic plants, is an important plant family to which it belongs. Another name for C. mukul is guggul. The primary component of this plant that is utilized as medicine is gum resin. There are references to the therapeutic value of guggul in ancient medical texts. It has been cited as a treatment for a number of illnesses in Ayurveda. Hypolipidemic, anti-obesity, antiinflammatory, antioxidant, anti-atherosclerotic, anti-arthritic, cardioprotective, antidiabetic, cytotoxic, hepatoprotective, thyroid stimulatory activity, antimicrobial, neuroprotective, antiacne, antipsoriatic, antifertility, antihemmorhoid, and antiurolithic properties are just a few of its pharmacological uses. Guggul is also utilized for a number of traditional, therapeutic, and spiritual purposes. Full of bioactive components, this plant has a rich phytochemical profile. The essential chemical components of guggul that have a number of medicinal applications are guggulsterones. Sugars, lignans, guggulsterols, terpenoids, steroids, flavonoids, and amino acids are other chemical constituents. It is in high demand in the pharmaceutical industry due to its many health benefits. Because of overexploitation, it is now in danger of extinction. Commiphora mukul's phytochemical profile and range of medicinal applications are described in this article(Sunita *et al.,* 2023).

The two main components of Gum Guggulu, one of the Divyaushidhi in Ayurveda, Guggulsterone-E and Guggulsterone-Z, have enormous therapeutic potential. The oleo-gum-resin of Commiphora wightii (Guggul), a severely endangered medicinal plant of the desert region, contains phytosterols known as guggulsterones. Research indicates that guggulsterones can be used to treat a variety of conditions, including cancer, obesity, arthritis, hyperlipidemia, hypercholesterolemia, and more. This paper discusses the plant's global distribution, the origin of gum guggulu, guggulsterones, their function in clinical biology, and potential phytosterol biosynthesis pathways that could help identify the as-yet-unidentified guggulsterone biosynthesis mechanism(Mehra & Kant, 2021).

Commiphora wightii (Arnott.) is a slow-growing, dioecious, balsamic tree of to the Burseraceae family that is mostly found in Bangladesh, Pakistan, and India's desert regions. C. wightii can be grown in the states of Rajasthan, Gujarat, Assam, Madhya Pradesh, and Karnataka. Since ancient times, C. wightii, also referred to as "Guggul," has been used to cure a wide range of ailments and issues because the oleo-gum resin contains the steroidal component guggulsterone. The effects of guggulsterone on lipid and cholesterol levels are mostly caused by its bioactive isomers E and Z. Additionally, recent studies have shown anticancer properties.Guggul grows slowly and takes years to bloom, making it a bad candidate for social forestry. Among other forest products, this shrub is used to make gum-resin and firewood. Its unrelenting exploitation and lack of conservation efforts have resulted in its inclusion on the International Union for Conservation of Nature's list of endangered plant species. Field surveys conducted over the past few decades have shown a decline in its wild population, and improper harvesting for its oleo-gum resin causes it to die after two to three years. This chapter provides an overview of the natural compound, pharmaceutical demand, conservation, and future research directions for this significant endangered medicinal plant(Akhter & Javed, 2023).

ORANGE PEEL – SOURCE OF CELLULOSE

Bioplastics are made from natural resources such as food waste, biomass, maize starch, and sugarcane bagasse. They are either fully or partially biodegradable in contrast to plastics made from fossil fuels. Bioplastics are therefore comparatively less detrimental to the environment. Bioplastics based on cellulose and starch are already utilized in straws, bowls, cutlery and packaging. Their performance and cost are not comparable to that of traditional plastics. The goal of the current study was to turn food waste into bioplastic. Orange peel is therefore selected because to its high cellulose content and convenient availability. Utilizing basic laboratory methods, the bio-plastic film made from orange peel was created. The new area of effort is identifying it for possible uses. Results from the produced film mixes using glycerol as a plasticizer have been consistent and encouraging. This material has a rough surface, has outstanding strength, flexibility, and disintegration under soiling circumstances and validates the biodegradability of the film. The developed material's physicochemical and surface morphology were confirmed to be bio-based plastic by characterization techniques including Fourier transform infrared (FTIR) spectroscopy, thermal gravimetric analysis (TGA), powder X-ray diffraction (XRD), and scanning electron microscopy (SEM). The production of bio-based plastic is explained as a straightforward, innovative and cost-effective technique(Yaradoddi *et al.,* 2022).

The production of value-adding products from waste materials is receiving increasing attention. Food waste is not only a significant global issue but it is also a great source of bioactive compounds. In this study, the parameters that affect the extraction of the bioactive compounds (polyphenols, ascorbic acid, hesperidin and carotenoids) from orange peels and their antioxidant properties were optimized using response surface methodology (RSM). The extraction temperature, time and solvent composition. Additionally, the effects of two additional techniques ultrasound (US) and pulsed electric field (PEF) either separately or in combination to see if they can improve the extraction of the compounds. The orange peels are a great source of numerous bioactive substances since the extracts included ascorbic acid (1228.93 mg/100 g dw), total polyphenols (34.71 mg GAE/g dw), hesperidin (16.26 mg/g dw) and total carotenoids (52.98 µg CtE/g dw)(Athanasiadis *et al.,* 2022).

Approximately 30 to 50 percent of food is wasted after harvest before being consumed. Fruit peels, pomace, seeds and other byproducts are common instances of food waste. Of these matrices a tiny percentage are valorized for bioprocessing, but the majority are still dumped in landfills. The manufacture of bioactive compounds and nanofillers from food by-products is a viable method to valorize them in this context. These products can then be utilized to functionalize biobased packaging materials. The goal of this study was to develop an effective technology for separating cellulose from orange peel residue during juice processing and turning it into cellulose nanocrystals (CNCs) for use in packaging goods' bionanocomposite sheets. Orange CNCs were used as reinforcing agents to chitosan/hydroxypropyl methylcellulose (CS/HPMC) films enhanced with lauroyl arginate ethyl (LAE®) after being evaluated by TEM and XRD studies. The impact of CNCs and LAE® on the functional and technical properties of CS/HPMC films was assessed. With an aspect ratio of 12.5 and average length and width of 500 nm and 40 nm, respectively, CNCs showed needle-like forms. Infrared spectroscopy and scanning electron microscopy verified the CS/HPMC blend's excellent compatibility with CNCs and LAE®. The addition of CNCs decreased the films' water solubility while increasing their tensile strength, light barrier, and water vapor barrier qualities. By adding LAE®, the films became more flexible and had biocidal activity against Salmonella enterica, Pseudomonas fluorescens, Escherichia coli, and Listeria monocytogenes—the primary bacterial pathogens that cause foodborne disease(Bigi *et al.,* 2023).

CORN FLOUR – SOURCE OF THERMOPLASTIC STARCH

The properties of the edible coating solutions (viscosity, pH, emulsion stability, oil droplets) and edible film (moisture content, contact angle, thermal properties, surface microscopy) were assessed. The solutions were made using the Pickering emulsion method and contained pregelatinized cornstarch (PCS), basil essential oil (BEO), and cellulose nanofibers (CNF). Using the dipping method, these solutions were applied to a mandarin orange and the quality parameters (weight loss, surface color, citric acid, tartaric acid, ascorbic acid and pH) were assessed after 12 days of storage at room temperature. 4% and 5% were the pregelatinized corn starch formulations 2% and 3% were the basil essential oil formulations and 0.5% was the cellulose nanofiber formulation. The pregelatinized corn starch and basil essential oil combination might be improved upon in order to preserve the quality of the mandarin orange fruit. The weight loss of the coated fruits was 19.81% and 20.11% respectively, compared to 24.41% for the control, indicating that the BEO3PCS4 and BEO3PCS5 treatments in particular were promising for extending the shelf life of the mandarin oranges. Regarding quality preservation, the color L* of the fruit surface was higher than 53.01 percent in the control, specifically on the final day of storage, at 54.78% (BEO3PCS4) and 56.73% (BEO3PCS5)(Wigati *et al.,* 2023).

Films made from starch have been extensively studied due to their affordability and degradability. Evaluation of the impact of protein fibril addition, particularly the amount and shape of fibrils, on the characteristics of starch-based films was the goal of this study. In order to create corn starch/whey protein isolate fibrils (CS/WPIF) films, CS was applied at pH 2.0 or 7.0 with varying WPIF levels (0.2%, 0.4%, and 0.6%). In order to modify the morphology of WPIF, the pH was changed to 2.0 or 7.0. Transmission electron microscopy revealed that the WPIF at pH 2.0 was longer than that at pH 7.0. When WPIF was added to CS films at pH 2.0 or 7.0, the films' tensile strength, relative crystallinity, and storage modulus increased while their water content, total soluble matter content, and water vapor permeability decreased. The strong network structure of the long fibrils at pH 2.0 enhanced the functional qualities of CS films more than the short fibrils at pH 7.0. WPIF at 0.6% decreased the film performance, possibly as a result of the aggregation of excessive WPIF, while CS/WPIF films with 0.4% WPIF showed the finest qualities. Additionally, CS/WPIF films prevented fresh-cut apples from browning while being stored and shown exceptional antioxidant qualities(Zheng *et al.,* 2024).

Edible film is a thin film matrix that is frequently used for food packaging and has particular flexible qualities. Films preserve food and extend the shelf life of products by acting as a barrier against mass transfer of substances like moisture, oxygen, light, lipids, and solutes. Starch is the most widely utilized form of polysaccharide among those used in edible films. Corn, potatoes, rice, cassava, tapioca and sweet potatoes are some of the frequently used sources of starch. While starch-based films have low mechanical qualities, they have good gas barriers. In order to improve the mechanical capabilities of edible films, several researchers have effectively altered their structure by adding co-biopolymers or other additives like plasticizers or natural extracts. Therefore, it is crucial for future research on the creation of edible films based on starch to comprehend the process underlying these parameters. Making changes to the film solution and casting it into a thin layer is how edible film is formed. After concentrating on the usage of different kinds of starch as a film or coating material, this article goes into great detail on the properties of the film and how it is used on fresh meat and meat products(Rahmadi Putri *et al.,* 2023).

Food packaging made of renewable materials lessens the environmental impact of conventional plastics while also assisting in the reduction of our reliance on fossil fuels. Since starch is inexpensive, widely available and has good film-forming qualities, it has become a hot issue in contemporary study. A thorough examination in this area is still missing, though. In the food business, starch-based films present a viable substitute for environmentally friendly packaging. The sources of raw materials, methods of modification, and mechanisms of film production are just a few of the topics covered in this study. Bridging the gap between research and real-world implementation requires an understanding of the physicochemical qualities and possible commercial applications. The use of starch-based films in the food business is finally covered in full. Various starch changes can enhance the films' mechanical and barrier qualities. Films made of starch can be given additional uses by adding active ingredients. Future research should therefore further examine and optimize these aspects in order to enhance the physicochemical characteristics and functioning of films based on starch. In conclusion, this analysis offers thorough details and the most recent advancements in the culinary industry's research on starch-based films(Wang *et al.,* 2024).

As environmental concerns and consumer awareness grow, there is a growing emphasis on edible, biodegradable and environmentally friendly food packaging films and coatings as a partial or complete replacement for traditional petroleum-based plastics. This chapter provides an overview of the uses of starch-based films in the food packaging sector. The starch molecule's high amylose concentration has been found to be the cause of its exceptional film-forming ability since amylose can crystallize. Starch-based films do have some drawbacks, though, such as a higher degree of hydrophilicity, which is the ability to change the film's mechanical and physicochemical properties by either increasing or decreasing its water content. The molecular level of nanoengineering, multilayer production, nanocomposite films, starch supply, rheological characteristics, and manufacturing process must also be comprehended. Through chemical treatment, the hydroxyl groups of starch molecules are changed, modifying the starch granules(Priyadarshini *et al.,* 2022).

By decreasing moisture loss, controlling respiration rate, enhancing surface smoothness or inhibiting microbiological development during storage, edible films and coatings offer a potentially useful way to preserve fresh food goods. Simultaneously, starch has demonstrated its affordability, non-toxicity and accessibility for use in the manufacturing of films and coatings. Nevertheless, this biopolymer has certain drawbacks when it comes to food preservation films. Because of this, additives are frequently used in its synthesis. This review focuses on how additives affect the bioactive qualities and physicochemical barriers of starch-based biodegradable polymer films and coatings. It also examines how these composites meet the standards needed to create edible and biodegradable food-based films and coatings. At a regulated rate these biopolymers can be added to packaged foods and work amazingly well as carriers for active compounds that have been separated from natural sources. In the films or coating, the additives also showed antibacterial and antioxidant properties, which would increase the coating's or packaged food's shelf durability. As a result, there is a lot of interest in the natural and eco-friendly edible films and coatings made from starch(Majeed *et al.,* 2023).

GLYCERINE – PLASTICIZER IN BIO FILM

It is well recognized that phenolic compounds with antioxidant qualities found in grape seed oil (Vitis vinivera L.) can be utilized as cosmetics, particularly for skincare. Glycerin has been used as a plasticizer and grape seed oil as an active ingredient to create a peel-off kind of emulgel mask. The purpose of this investigation was to ascertain how the plasticizer glycerin affected the stability and physical characteristics of the grape seed oil emulgel mask composition over time. An emulsion is first created, and it is subsequently mixed with the Hydroxypropyl Methyl Cellulose (HPMC) gel base to create the emulgel. Five different glycerin concentrations were used to create the formulations. Over the course of four weeks, the organoleptic and other physical parameters were evaluated at two different temperatures (25 °C and 40 °C). Glycerin's function as a plasticizer led to the evaluation of elongation and tensile strength tests. The physical stability statistical analysis revealed that none of the formulations differed significantly. The mask dries in ten to twenty-five minutes on average. Tensile strength revealed notable variations between formulations, although elongation test results revealed no discernible differences. According to the findings of the aforementioned investigation, glycerine, when used as a plasticizer, has an impact on the grape seed oil peel-off emulgel mask's appearance but no discernible influence on the preparation's physical stability or qualities(Nursal *et al.,* 2021).

The unidirectional freeze casting process was used to create aligned porous scaffolds from soy protein amyloid fibrils that had been plasticized with glycerin. It was examined how the amount of glycerin affected the SAFs-Gly scaffolds' structural and functional characteristics. Scanning electron microscopy verified that altering the quantity of glycerin may modify the scaffolds' aligned pore size and distribution, with diameters ranging from 10 to 50 μm. The scaffolds' median pore size shrank and the strain at the yield point rose by as much as 40% when the glycerin concentration was raised. Furthermore, the scaffolds' water resistance considerably improved without causing any discernible morphological alterations. . Two glass transitions in the SAFs/glycerin systems were identified by differential scanning calorimetry analysis; these corresponded to the protein-rich and glycerin-rich domains, respectively. FTIR spectroscopy showed that SAFs and glycerin formed intermolecular hydrogen bonds and hydroxyl interactions. Glycerin may be able to partially induce SAFs crystallization, structural separation, and β-sheet exfoliation, according to X-ray diffraction and small-angle X-ray scattering. These outcomes show how this method can be used in the food sector and will likely be applied in the creation of food-based polymer scaffolds(Shan *et al.,* 2024).

CONCLUSION

Edible coating derived from agro-waste represents an innovative and sustainable approach to enhance the shelf life, quality, and safety of fresh fruits. The utilization of agricultural by-products such as fruit peels, vegetable residues, cereal husks, and plant fibers provides an eco-friendly alternative to synthetic packaging materials, contributing to waste valorization and environmental conservation. These bio-based coatings not only act as a physical barrier to moisture loss, microbial contamination, and oxidation but also improve the nutritional and functional properties of fruits due to the presence of bioactive compounds like antioxidants, antimicrobials, and polyphenols naturally present in agro-waste.Despite the promising benefits, challenges remain in achieving desirable mechanical properties, transparency, and consumer acceptability of agro-waste-based edible coatings. Further research is required to optimize coating formulations, improve their stability, and develop cost-effective processing techniques suitable for commercial applications. Innovations such as incorporating nanotechnology, essential oils, and biodegradable polymers can further enhance the effectiveness of these coatings.

In conclusion, edible coatings from agro-waste hold significant potential in sustainable food preservation strategies, aligning with global trends toward green technology and circular economy. Their application not only reduces post-harvest losses but also promotes environmental sustainability, offering a promising future for safe, natural, and functional food packaging solutions.

REFERENCE

1. Saeed, M., Azam, M., Saeed, F., Arshad, U., Afzaal, M., Bader Ul Ain, H., Ashraf, J., & Nasir, Z. (2021). Development of antifungal edible coating for strawberry using fruit waste. *Journal of Food Processing and Preservation*, 45(11), e15956.
2. Kumar, P., Sethi, S., Sharma, R. R., Singh, S., & Varghese, E. (2023). Edible coatings enriched with plant-based extracts preserve postharvest quality of fruits: A review. *Progress in Organic Coatings*, 182, 107669.
3. Kumar, N., & Basu, S. (2023). Recent advances in the preservation of postharvest fruits using edible films and coatings: A comprehensive review. *Food Chemistry*, 418, 135916.
4. de Oliveira Filho, J. G., Albiero, B. R., Oldoni, F. C. A., Vellosa, J. C. R., & Egea, M. B. (2019). Development and evaluation of a film and edible coating obtained from the *Cajanus cajan* seed applied to fresh strawberry fruit. *Food and Bioprocess Technology*, 12, 1090–1101
5. Gutiérrez, T. J. (2023). Edible coatings and films for shelf-life extension of fruit and vegetables. *Biomaterials Advances*, 154, 213632.
6. Zhang, W., Jiang, H., Rhim, J.-W., & Cao, J. (2023). Recent advances in polysaccharide-based edible coatings for preservation of fruits and vegetables: A review. *Critical Reviews in Food Science and Nutrition*, 64(12), 2001–2021.
7. Romanazzi, G., Sanzani, S. M., Bi, Y., Tian, S., Gutiérrez-Pérez, O., & Alkan, N. (2023). Chitosan and other edible coatings to extend shelf life, manage postharvest decay, and reduce loss and waste of fresh fruits and vegetables. *Trends in Food Science & Technology*, 132, 270–281.
8. Singh, T., & Kaur, A. (2022). Biopolymer based edible coating for enhancing the shelf life of horticulture products. *Food Chemistry: Molecular Sciences*, 4, 100085.
9. Pascual, L., Llorca, E., & Pérez-Masiá, R. (2023). Edible coatings as a natural packaging system to improve fruit and vegetable shelf life and quality. *International Journal of Molecular Sciences*, 24(19), 14645.
10. Lin, D., & Zhao, Y. (2007). Innovations in the development and application of edible coatings for fresh and minimally processed fruits and vegetables. *Comprehensive Reviews in Food Science and Food Safety*, 6(3), 60–75

CHAPTER 10

Significance of Cutting Force and Temperature Rise in End Milling Process

Sethupathy A
Assistant Professor, Dept. of Mechanical Engineering, SNS College of Technology, Coimbatore, Tamil Nadu

Manufacturing industries use metal cutting as a method to modify raw materials geometry to create mechanical parts. A wedge-shaped tool is used to remove extra material from a workpiece in the form of a chip during the metal cutting process. The cost of machining operations is a major factor to increase profitability. Industries searching for effective technology to produce a product at a faster rate but at a lower cost without compromising the product qualities. The selection of appropriate machining parameters is the most important factor in any machining operation design process. Work piece parameters and machine settings are the most important factors that influence machinability qualities. The thermal effect of machining operation is important other factor which influences the efficiency of machining process. Optimizing the process tool parameters and machine parameters must be the optimal objective of any machining process to minimize the time as well as to improve the machine economics. The cost of machining is referred to as machining economics. Energy, capital expenditure, labor, and equipment are all inputs to any manufacturing system. To improve the machine economics, the production cost, surface roughness, force used for cutting, tool wear, rate of metal removal must be at minimum rate and the rate of production and tool life must be at maximum rate.

The manufacturing processes like turning, milling, boring, drilling, are out of date process commonly used to remove materials. In the aforementioned processes, metal is separated as a plastically partial chip of metal. Various technological advancements have had a considerable impact on metal cutting operations. A machine tool, a control system, and a cutting tool are the three main components of the modern metal removal process. Machining is often carried out utilizing dedicated, particularly developed machining systems for large production, resulting in a massive revolution in metal cutting practice. The creation of novel tooling materials, as well as the emergence of flexible, agile, or reconfigurable machining structures based on high-tech numeric control machine tools, are all great consequences of today's degree of progress in the metal cutting area.

In metal cutting operation, extra metal is removed by pushing the work piece against a revolving multi-point tool in milling. Recently, end milling is widely used technology for metal cutting process by various manufacturing industries. The focus of this study is to understand the machining process in CNC end mill to machine selected aluminum (Al 7075) composite using end mill cutter made up of high-speed steel. To ensure machining economics, tool geometries like cutting speed, rate of feed and depth of cut must be chosen effectively. To identify the best conditions, a machinability test and a process simulation might be employed. The impact of machining factors such as helix angle, radial rake angle, cutting tool nose radius, cutting speed, feed rate, and axial depth of cut on machining performance is examined.

END-MILLING PROCESS

End-milling is a sort of peripheral milling operation used for technical purposes including profiling and slotting. End milling is a multipoint, intermittent cutting method in which the cutting edge does not maintain constant contact with the workpiece and the uncut chip thickness differs with spindle revolution. Milling is widely employed in the industry, and milled metals are frequently used in manufacturing industries, die, aviation, car, assets and systems and equipment design. End milling creates contours, slots, etches, bends, and grooves in a variety of components. Since the introduction of computer-aided numerical control milling, milling operations have been more cost-effective and efficient over time.

This technology is used to produce flat surfaces, curved profiles, and different other intricate designs with excellent precision and a high level of surface finish. Moulds, dies, the automobile and aerospace sectors all use end milling extensively. This process is particularly common in the aircraft industry due to the precision and complexity required in the final measurements. The usage of computerized numerical control milling has improved the competency and productivity of milling processes.

Milling cutters are available in many types of shapes and sizes, and they are used for a variety of operations. End-mill cutters have teeth on one end of the circumferential surface. There are two types of shanks: straight and tapered. It has helical or parallel teeth to the rotational axis. An end mill with a modest helix angle is known as a spiral end mill.

Milling is the process of removing metal by passing it through a spinning multi toothed cutter. The material removal rate is increased during this operation because the cutter revolves at a rapid cutting speed. The multi cutting edges of the milling cutter improve the surface quality as well. The milling cutter works in a completely different way than a drill or a turning tool. Milling is a sporadic process in which each tooth makes a chip of a different thickness, whereas the turning and drilling keep the cutting tool in continuous contact with the workpiece to be cut.
End-mill cutters produce two workpiece surfaces at the same time, with cutting edges on both the end-face and the cutter body's periphery. They are often used in operations such as facing, profiling, slotting, and plunging. Solid high-speed steel (HSS), cobalt enriched high-speed steels (HSS-Co), solid carbide tools, sintered tungsten carbide (WC), ceramic, polycrystalline diamond (PCD), inserted blade, and indexable insert design are some of the materials used. In addition, end-milling is used to create profiles, slots, engraves, curves, and pockets in a variety of parts.

The milling process is exposed to vibration and chatter due to high impact loads at the entrance and varying cutting force. Spring back and the chatter is two of the most common difficulties with end mill cutters that are connected to stiffness. Spring back is produced by a lack of stiffness in the cutter, which results in deflection or distortion of the cutter as a result of cutting forces. During tool retraction chatter can occur which leads to scratch marks due to extreme elastic recovery of the end mill cutter. The ratio of length to diameter (or overhang) of a cutter determines its resonance frequencies and chatter resistance and the overhang ratios greater than four or five are highly susceptible to chatter. This factor has a significant impact on milling cutter design.

Cutting tool geometry such as helix angle, rake angle, relief angle, nose radius and machining parameters like spindle speed, feed rate, and depth-of-cut have a significant impact on machining performance (Gowthaman and Jagadeesha, 2020). Incorrectly calculated machining parameters and a poorly designed cutting tool not only decrease surface quality but also increase cutting forces, impacting stability and creating thermal deformation due to temperature rise fluctuations at the cutting zone and high tool wear.

End mill cutters made up of High-speed steel material with a standard 35°helix angle in five different radial rake angles and nose radius was selected to conduct the trials in this study. The machining performance based on the radial rake angles and nose radius has been investigated and analyzed. Aluminum alloy (Al 7075 – T6) was chosen as the workpiece material.

ALUMINUM ALLOY (AL7075- T6)

Aluminum-7075 series alloy is a zinc-based alloy which generally utilized in numerous applications in all types of manufacturing industries because of its unique mechanical properties with low density and high strength. It has great mechanical qualities such as superior ductility, strength, toughness, and fatigue resistance. When compared to most of the other alloys, it is more easily subjected to embrittlement because of its micro segregation. It has more corrosion resistance when compared to other 2000 series alloys. It's one of the most extensively used aluminum alloys for high-stress structural applications, and it's used in many aircraft structural parts.

The aluminum alloy is used as a continuous phase which is reinforced with single and multiple reinforcement particulates such as SiC, Al_2O_3, Gr, TiO_2, B_4C, AlN, fly ash, and other materials to create composites with higher strength than the base alloy material. The composite models have emerging requirements in fast-growing technologies in different manufacturing industries (Imran and Khan, 2019). T6 temper 7075 has a yield strength of at least 430–480 MPa (63,000–69,000 psi) and ultimate tensile strength of 510–540 MPa (74,000–78,000 psi). It has a 5–11 per cent failure elongation. Hence, AL 7075-T6 is selected for this present study. Table 1.1 gives the chemical composition of AL 7075-T6 aluminum alloy.

Table 1.1 Chemical composition of AL7075-T6 aluminum alloy

Element	Composition (%)
Al	87.1- 91.4
Zn	5.1- 6.1
Mg	2.1- 2.9
Cu	1.2- 2
Fe	Max- 0.5
Cr	0.18-0.28
Mn	Max- 0.3
Ti	Max- 0.2
Si	Max- 0.4

TOOL MATERIAL

High Speed Steel (HSS) is a self-hardening steel having a high degree of red hardness, strong abrasion resistance, and a similar degree of shock resistance. Their primary purpose is to be utilized as a cutting tool material. The material generally used for extrusion dies and blanking punches where dies are utilized various applications. Tungsten, molybdenum, chromium, and vanadium are the primary alloying elements with cobalt added in superior grades. The high-speed steels are more difficult to grind and process because of its high carbon and alloy content. The two types of high-speed steels are Tungsten high speed steels (T-type steels) and molybdenum high speed steels (M-type steels). The T-types are subjected to heat treatment more quickly in comparison with M-types, but less tough than M-type.

SIGNIFICANCE OF CUTTING FORCES IN END-MILLING

Predicting cutting forces in milling operations is critical for efficiently designing the machining process, by determining the right process parameters, tools, and fixtures. To minimize the quality issues such as tool deflection, chatter, or fixture can be minimized by effective cutting force. The efficient cutting force can also increase productivity. High cutting forces in milling are unfavourable because they result in poor surface smoothness, inaccurate measurements, and increased tool wear. Material machinability can be compared by measuring cutting force. It is also important to monitor cutting operation, tool wear and failure in real-time. The machine power requirements, bearing loads and fixture design can be calculated by estimating cutting force. The most current strategies for improving milling quality and efficiency include the ability to modify cutting parameters on the run to minimize chatter and optimize productivity.

Cutting forces created in metal cutting processes (Shubham *et al.* 2020) cause deflections of the part, tool (Agarwal and Desai, 2020) or machine structure, as well as provide energy to the machining system, resulting in high temperatures and unstable vibrations. In the milling process, high cutting forces cause poor surface finish, incorrect measurements and increased tool wear (Tihabadiral *et al.* 2019). Infeed force (axial direction force) is the cutting force in the X-direction. Crossfeed force is the cutting force in the Y direction (radial direction force). The thrust force is the cutting force in the Z direction (tangential direction force) (Zhang, 2002).

SIGNIFICANCE OF TEMPERATURE RISE IN END-MILLING

Cutting tools, on the other hand, are subject to the rubbing process in machining. High-temperature rise is caused by scrubbing between the workpiece materials and the cutting tool. In the metal cutting process, much of the power consumed is converted into heat near the tool's cutting edge. This heating process directly or indirectly causes many technical issues and economic challenges.

The machining cost is highly influenced by the rate of metal removal. The cost can be decreased by raising the cutting speed and/or feed rate. However, there are speed and feed limits beyond which the tool's life is drastically shortened. When the metal removal rate is high, the tools are heated to a high temperature and it leads to the melting of metals and alloys. Above certain critical speeds, due to stress and temperature, the tools tend to collapse in a short cutting duration (Kiprawi *et al.* 2019). As a result, it's critical to comprehend the components that govern heat creation, heat movement, and heat storage.

High temperature is produced in the deformation regions and outlying areas of the chip, tool, and workpiece surface by the heat energy. This increase in temperature causes tool wear, degrades workpiece quality and raises tooling costs. The work material properties are affected by temperature rise, as a moderate temperature rise leads to residual tension in the surface of the workpiece whilst a high temperature may lead to hardness of workpiece material. When milling, a cutting tool with high hardness at room temperature is impossible to maintain that hardness at high temperatures.

The temperature rises in the rake surface of the tool significantly influence the tool wear rate. The tool softens and wears more quickly as the temperature in this location rises. As the temperature increases, the tool material disperses into chips and results in tool failure. When the workpiece material sticks to the tools due to high temperature, the tool softens which leads to rapid wear. Identifying the temperature's critical value is vital for tool wear reduction. The temperature rise on the tool's relief face affects the surface quality and metallurgical state of the workpiece surface.

CONCLUSION

Manufacturing of components with complex profiles, end milling is the most used metal removal method in the automobile and valve sectors. High-speed metal cutting causes workpiece distortion, increased cutting forces, and a high temperature rise at the tool-workpiece contact. Predicting these responses, which have an impact on the quality of machining in end milling, is crucial. The study investigated the influence of tool and machining parameters on the measured responses of end mill and prediction and optimization of outcome in terms of machining parameters

References

1. Abukhshim, NA, Mativenga, PT & Sheikh, MA 2006, 'Heat generation and temperature prediction in metal cutting: A review and implications for high speed machining', International Journal of Machine Tools & Manufacture, vol. 46, no. 7-8, pp. 782-800.
2. Anayet, MD, Patwari1, U, Nurul Amin, AKM & Waleed, F, 2009, 'Prediction of tangential cutting force in end milling of medium carbon steel by coupling design of experiment and response surface methodology', Journal of Mechanical Engineering, vol. 40, no. 2, pp. 95-103.
3. Andreas Hilligardt, Felicitas Böhland, Jan Klose, Michael Gerstenmeyer & Volker Schulze 2021, 'A new approach for local cutting force modeling enabling the transfer between different milling conditions and tool geometries', scientific committee of the 18th CIRP Conference on Modeling of Machining Operation. 10.1016/j.procir.2021.09.024.
4. Ansalam Raj, TG & Narayanan, VN & Namboothiri 2010, 'An Improved genetic algorithm for the prediction of surface finish in dry turning of SS 420 materials', Int J Adv Manuf Technol, vol.47, pp.313–324.
5. Balkrishna Rao, Chinmaya, R, Dandekar, Yung, C & Shin 2011, 'An experimental and numerical study on the face milling of Ti–6Al–4V alloy: Tool performance and surface integrity', Journal of Materials Processing Technology, vol. 211, no.2, pp. 294-304.
6. Balkrishna, R, Chinmaya, R, Dandekar, R, Yung, C & Shin 2011, 'An experimental and numerical study on the face milling of Ti–6Al–4V alloy: Tool performance and surface integrity', Journal of Materials Processing Technology, vol. 211, pp. 294–304.
7. Bin, F, Zhonghang, Y, Depeng, LI, Liying, G 2021, 'Effect of ultrasonic vibration on finished quality in ultrasonic vibration assisted micromilling of Inconel718', Chinese Journal of Aeronautics, vol.34, pp. 209 - 219.
8. Bolar, G, Das, A, Joshi, SN 2018, 'Measurement and analysis of cutting force and product surface quality during end-milling of thin-wall components', Journal of Measurement, vol. 121, pp. 190 -204.
9. Boopale, R. Pawade, S, Joshi 2015, 'Surface quality analysis in ball end milling of Inconel 718 cantilevers by response surface methodology', J. of Eng. Manuf, DOI:10.1177/ 0954405415600140.
10. Botko, F, Hatala, M, Duplak, J, Olexa, I, Birčak, J 2018, 'Study of High Feed Cutting Efficiency of Aluminum Alloy AW' – Alzn5,5mgcu, SAR journal science and research issue, vol. 2, pp. 53-56.

FSC
www.fsc.org
MIX
Papier | Fördert
gute Waldnutzung
FSC® C083411

Kolibri 360 GmbH
Ferdinand-Jühlke-Straße 7
99095 Erfurt, Deutschland
produktsicherheit@kolibri360.de

Druck:
CPI Druckdienstleistungen GmbH
im Auftrag der
Kolibri 360 GmbH
Ferdinand-Jühlke-Str. 7
99095 Erfurt